RECONCILABLE
DIFFERENCES

RECONCILABLE DIFFERENCES

U.S.-French Relations in the New Era

MICHAEL BRENNER

GUILLAUME PARMENTIER

BROOKINGS INSTITUTION PRESS
Washington, D.C.

Library of Congress Cataloging-in-Publication Data

Brenner, Michael J.
Reconcilable differences : U.S.-French relations in the new era /
Michael Brenner and Guillaume Parmentier.
p.   cm.
Includes bibliographical references and index.
ISBN 0-8157-1254-5 (cloth)— ISBN 0-8157-1253-7 (paper)
1. United States—Foreign relations—France.   2. France—Foreign
relations—United States.   3. United States—Foreign relations—1989–
4. Political culture—United States.   5. Political culture—France.
6. National characteristics, American.   7. National characteristics,
French.   I. Parmentier, Guillaume.   II. Title.
E183.8.F8 B74 2002   2001007583
327.73044—dc21   CIP

Typeset in Minion

Composition by R. Lynn Rivenbark
Macon, Georgia

Printed by R. R. Donnelley and Sons
Harrisonburg, Virginia

The Brookings Institution is an independent organization devoted to nonpartisan research, education, and publication in economics, government, foreign policy, and the social sciences generally. Its principal purposes are to aid in the development of sound public policies and to promote public understanding of issues of national importance. The Institution was founded on December 8, 1927, to merge the activities of the Institute for Government Research, founded in 1916, the Institute of Economics, founded in 1922, and the Robert Brookings Graduate School of Economics and Government, founded in 1924. The Institution maintains a position of neutrality on issues of public policy to safeguard the intellectual freedom of the staff.

To Lucie
To Maya

Foreword

FRENCH-AMERICAN RELATIONS often seem synonymous with trans-atlantic frictions. For a whole range of historical, cultural, and strategic rea-sons—all well explained in this book—the two countries have often clashed on issues ranging from NATO to trade to the Middle East. While some of the old issues that used to divide us—colonial wars and the management of the cold war, for example—are no longer relevant, the new era has brought with it new French-American debates, such as over the merits and drawbacks of an American-led "unipolar world." Even as the world context changes, it often seems that France and the United States, two ambitious global powers that often see themselves as models for others, are fated to clash.

At the same time the two countries share core convictions about build-ing a stable world order grounded on principles of democracy. Their ability to cooperate has been evident most recently in bringing peace to the Balkans, promoting constructive ties to Russia, and now in the war on ter-rorism. The fact that each country can be useful to the other challenges leaders in both Washington and Paris to manage their conflicts while more fully realizing their potential to work effectively together. France's key role within the European Union, which is developing more and more into a major force on the world scene, makes French-American understanding even more imperative.

This book is a valuable attempt to look at the basis for that potential understanding in the new era that began with the end of the cold war and now enters a new phase after the terrorist attacks of September 11, 2001. While there have been many books written about French-American rela-tions, this one is unique in the way it seeks to place the old debates in the context of the new era and provides a careful examination of the political, economic, and security debates the two countries have managed throughout the 1990s and into the new century.

The study was done in the context of two new policy centers, the Center on the United States and France (CUSF) at Brookings and the French Center on the United States (CFE) at the French Institute for International Relations (IFRI) in Paris. As important as France is to the United States across a whole range of policy issues, there was curiously not a great deal of policy-relevant research being done on the French-American relationship in the United States. And as important as the United States is in French foreign policy, French scholars were not actually focusing on American politics and foreign relations in a systematic way. The creation of the two centers was an attempt to help fill these gaps. In this book, Guillaume Parmentier, the head of the CFE in Paris, teamed up with Michael Brenner, a leading American expert on France, Europe, and American foreign policy, to produce what I think is an outstanding assessment of the new French-American relationship and the many issues that make it so important.

The authors would like to thank Richard N. Haass, then director of the Foreign Policy Studies program at Brookings, who commissioned this study and who played such a critical role in the establishment of the two centers. They are grateful to Philip H. Gordon, Brookings senior fellow and director of the CUSF, for his comments on the manuscript and help in shepherding it through the review process. They also warmly thank Simon Serfaty and several anonymous reviewers for their careful reading of the original manuscript. Helpful research assistance was provided by Jacques Beltran, Barthelémy Courmont, Daniel Keohane, and Elizabeth Ramborger. Special thanks are due to Ashley Milkop for his research assistance and for his compiling and rereading the work in the final stages. Finally, a word of thanks to Janet Mowery, whose careful copy editing ensured a seamless integration of the work of two authors working on opposite sides of the Atlantic, and to Vicki Chamlee and Mary Mortensen, who proofread and indexed the pages.

The authors and all of us at Brookings are also grateful to the German Marshall Fund of the United States for its support of this project.

The views expressed here are solely those of the authors and should not be attributed to any person or organization acknowledged above or to the trustees, officers, or other staff members of the Brookings Institution.

MICHAEL H. ARMACOST
President, Brookings Institution

February 2002
Washington, D.C.

Contents

RECONCILABLE
DIFFERENCES

CHAPTER ONE

A Unique Partnership

THE U.S.-FRENCH RELATIONSHIP is a unique mix of rivalry and cooperation. Historical allies and comrades in arms, the United States and France are often fractious and quarrelsome.[1] These visions are not irreconcilable, however. Even if a divorce were possible, there would be insufficient grounds to support it. French-American frictions are a staple of transatlantic relations, so much so that it is easy to dismiss them as a stylized family feud whose manifestations are tempered by the absence of fundamental conflict. In our estimation, such a complacent assessment is mistaken. The fundamental changes that have taken place since 1989 have made tensions more serious because they are not contained by the tight configurations of the cold war.[2] Differences now have more room to play themselves out and can have wider repercussions. The tense and often contentious duel between Washington and Paris over a wide array of issues—designs for the new security architecture of Europe, for supervising commercial competition, for coping with the conflicts of the former Yugoslavia—all have had meaning and consequence that have gone well beyond the status of their bilateral relationship.[3]

France's European challenge to American domination in the early 1990s encapsulated two central issues: how to reconstitute the political space of postcommunist Europe and how to redistribute roles and responsibilities in the transatlantic partnership.[4] The expression of this ambition in an atmosphere made acrimonious by the clash of national egos generated tensions, though some of these proved eventually to be constructive. It would be a mistake to stereotype France's actions, though, to interpret the French strategy as nothing other than a vain campaign to regain a

1

standing incommensurate with its middle-power status. It would be equally wrong to ascribe to American policymakers an implacable insistence on preserving—indeed extending—an imperium at variance with the times and circumstances.

France's questioning of American dominance expressed more than an impulse to clip the wings of the American eagle. It brought to the surface the core question of what practical meaning was attached to the concept of "the West."[5] The existence of a Euro-Atlantic partnership rooted in shared values and mutual interests was not in question. Other propositions were less obviously valid. Should NATO, that partnership's embodiment as a military alliance, continue to be the main construct for organizing the transatlantic relationship? Was it the proper instrument for affirming a unified political strategy of the Western democracies? Indeed, was there compelling reason for them to organize themselves in formal concert when the enemy that had been the alliance's raison d'être no longer existed and Europe's ideological divide had been erased?

An implicit issue at the heart of French thinking was the measure of autonomy that should be granted distinctly Western European institutions—the European Union (EU) and the Western European Union (WEU)—in a balanced partnership. In such a partnership it was unclear what U.S. leadership prerogatives were still justified and what steps should be taken to ensure that Washington's voice would still be heard in the European forums when matters of interest to the United States were under consideration.[6] In the economic realm a debate was opening over what rules were needed for regulating commercial and financial markets, which were globalizing without commensurate development of authoritative mechanisms for their oversight. More broadly, there was the challenge of reconciling the allies' growing desire to leave their own diplomatic mark on the wider world agenda with the implied American claim to primacy and unique competence as the West's global standard-bearer.

French answers to these questions composed a vision of the post–cold war world that looked quite different from the reality at the time and was at variance with the model acquiring definition in the minds of Washington officials. These answers deserve close examination.

Of all the long-standing connections between allies in the Western world, the French-American relationship is undoubtedly the most unsteady. It is also one of the most important. Indeed, it largely defines what the West can and cannot do. Promoting rival strategies on how to manage the international system, all the while sensing that nothing can destroy their traditional friendship, the two countries have seemingly set their relationship on a perennial roller coaster. Their alliance, dating from America's founding and consecrated through the two world wars, seems to permit rather than inhibit sporadic outbreaks of ill temper. During the cold war, their sharp clashes never shook the core conviction that, in their enduring fraternity, the positive elements would always outweigh the negative ones. This truth held despite France's dramatic withdrawal from NATO's integrated command structure under Charles de Gaulle in 1966, which forced the alliance's military headquarters to move from Fontainebleau to Mons, in Belgium; their relationship also survived France's determined effort to divest the French treasury of dollar-denominated assets in exchange for gold bullion in a frontal challenge to dollar dominance of the postwar international monetary system.[7] The current tendency to depict present French-American relations as more troubled and fractious than at any other time lacks historical perspective. It is true that France and the United States differ over the desirable means and methods for maintaining a stable international order, especially over what the role of the United States should be. Still, these differences are reconcilable. Today's disagreements between Paris and Washington pale in comparison with those of the 1960s.

The French tendency to question the wisdom of American foreign policy sometimes springs from a vision of the United States as a clumsy parvenu on the world stage. This peculiarly French mistrust of U.S. foreign policy is based on a mixture of a historical legacy and more recent fears about perceived excesses of latter-day American power. Prominent French critics of the United States fix on this widespread unease about U.S. statecraft as much as on U.S. intentions. They are acutely sensitive to signs that France is following in the wake of a U.S. policy lead. The word *suivisme* (followership) used by critics on the left and right of the political spectrum is meant to be strongly pejorative. This persistent disparaging characterization of U.S. foreign policy notwithstanding, the French people's instinctive distrust of American aims and methods has weakened noticeably in recent years. Anti-Americanism is now the preserve of small, marginal groups on the right and the left and a handful of maverick intellectuals from an earlier era.[8]

The expression "hyper-puissance," coined by Foreign Minister Hubert Védrine, well illustrates these mixed French feelings of apprehension and respect. Védrine, like Jacques Chirac and unlike his former mentor, François Mitterrand, has a personal fascination with American politics and policy-making. He is dedicated to the improvement of French ties to Washington, a principal goal of his tenure at the Quai d'Orsay. This approach, which fits with the outlook of today's policy elite in Paris, is accompanied by accord with the overall objectives pursued by the United States. Its aim is to have the two countries work together to implement wisely considered policies to achieve these aims. As Védrine reiterates, candid criticism is a mark of friendship. By this measure, France is America's first friend.

The purpose of this study is to examine broadly the French-American relationship since the cold war. We show how national identity, political culture, and diplomatic style strain ties between Washington and Paris far more than conflicts of interest do. The emphasis is on the most salient events and their repercussions on bilateral dealings between Washington and Paris and on Euro-American relations generally.

Much of our analysis concentrates on the aspirations, achievements, and contradictions of French policy—and on the American response to it. The reason for this is twofold. First, there is more attentive French analysis of U.S. policies than American analysis of French policies. This circumstance reflects the lopsidedness of the relationship, with French interest in the United States often verging on obsession and American attention to France often verging on indifference. Because we are making a modest attempt to rectify this imbalance, the apportioning of space reflects the unequal attention devoted to each partner by the other. Second, this volume is aimed primarily at the American foreign policy community, where, by definition, knowledge of U.S. policies, as well as of its determining factors, can be taken as given. But knowledge of France in the United States is relatively thin because very few recent U.S. studies address current French policies, and understanding of French domestic policymaking as it affects foreign policy is scarcer still. We have therefore decided to devote substantial space to a description and analysis of these domestic elements in the hope that it will help readers better understand the parameters in which French foreign policy is made. They are to a large extent structural and unlikely to be modified fundamentally in the foreseeable future.

We have attempted to make this study as policy relevant as possible, in order to make a contribution to mutual understanding among decisionmakers and the influential public in each country. We treat the bilateral relationship as having its own logic and dynamics, yet one that is set within a wider framework of multilateral institutions. A deeper and more constructive dialogue between the two countries is essential to Europe's future well-being and the vitality of the transatlantic partnership.

Chapter 2, "Single Superpower versus Multipolarity," compares the countries' visions of the post–cold war world, juxtaposing the French multipolar model and the U.S. view of itself as the lone superpower with unique duties and prerogatives. The very different French and American foreign policy traditions complicate pulling into focus these two viewpoints. Chapter 3, "NATO: Lost Opportunities," concentrates on how and why the two nations often act at cross-purposes in the security field. It demonstrates how rival institutional models with antecedents in the cold war era posed insurmountable obstacles to devising a common strategy for building a comprehensive European security system. An opportunity was lost in the mid-1990s to reconcile the transatlantic vision of the United States and France's European project. Chapter 4, "High Tension: The Economic Dimension," extends the diagnosis into the domain of commercial rivalry. Here, too, contending interests are associated with the two nations' quite different conceptions of economic management, domestically and internationally, even if the stereotype of "dirigiste" France is no more valid than that of the United States as a perfect market. The European Union's role cuts both ways. It strengthens France's position by aligning other countries with its views, but it also requires France to bring itself nearer to the positions of its European partners. A subsection on the defense industry analyzes how both countries highly value the stakes in this sensitive sector. Chapter 5, "A Rekindled Alliance," examines the bilateral and multilateral tracks to follow in order to put the French-American relationship on a positive footing. The accent is on a forthright, better-structured dialogue between Washington and Paris. We stress the value of developing a dense network of exchanges among policymakers, political elites, and business leaders across the span of issues that trouble French-American relations. The key is a fuller understanding of the distinctive political ethos and political processes in each country. On that foundation, fruitful innovation in modes of cooperation becomes a realistic possibility. France would gain acknowledgment of its influence in European affairs and the space in which to exercise it constructively. The United States would gain confirmation of its status as a European power and a valuable partner in exercising its global leadership.

CHAPTER TWO

Single Superpower versus Multipolarity

THE POLITICAL UPHEAVAL that reshaped Europe's geostrategic map in 1989–90 rendered obsolete the cold war paradigms. Western governments were not presented, though, with a blank slate on which they could compose entirely new arrangements. Although the disintegrating political structures in the East required replacement, it was not obvious how they should be connected to the West's own institutional inheritance—for the multilateral institutions developed during the cold war had acquired an identity and value independent of their strategic context. That was to prove true for the North Atlantic Treaty Organization (NATO) as well as the European Community (EC). The search for new organizing constructs that preoccupied foreign policy elites in Washington and Paris centered on a reconsideration of the established architecture; the United States showed a strong preference for reconfirming NATO's primacy, and France promoted an expanded vision of the European Union (EU). The challenge had greater urgency in Paris than in Washington.

For the United States, its superpower status now unchallenged, the quandary was what to make of its success. What guideposts should be followed in deciding how to delimit the range of its power and commitments? On what basis should responsibilities be shared with allies in the absence of a major rival or a strategic threat? Would allies less in need of the American nuclear umbrella still defer to leadership from Washington?[1] Victory in the cold war punctuated the closing of an extraordinary chapter in American history. Its championing of the West in the global contest against Soviet communism drew strength and validity from its self-image as destiny's child born with a mission to bear the torch of political enlightenment. This was the hour of triumph for democracy and the free-market economy. Freedom had prevailed over a mortal ideological enemy as well as a dangerous military foe. For France the victory was seen as primarily geopolitical. Different lessons were drawn in the two countries from the collapse of the bipolar system. The United States felt deeply that the intrinsic superiority of the principles on which its liberal system is grounded had been the key factor ensuring the West's success. Consequently, U.S. leaders believed that they had renewed justification for presenting the American model as universally valid and the surest basis for building a new world order.[2] A world dominated by American ways and managed by American power was seen as benign and irresistible.

France's situation looked less enviable. Its international position was unsettled by the combination of Germany's reunification and the end to Europe's division. Strategic predestination had given way to strategic free will. This more challenging environment threatened France's disproportionate influence within the truncated Europe of the European Union; but it also created the opportunity to liberate its diplomacy from America's hegemonic grip and to promote "Europe" in the councils of the West and on the world stage.

The Power of History

France, the country of the French Revolution, believes that it has a special place among the nations, as well as a special message to convey, and that therefore it enjoys a special place in the appreciation of other peoples. In particular, it believes it played a key role in "helping" peoples resist foreign tyranny. That belief is a source of great national pride. The French, not unlike the Americans, are convinced that they are popular abroad.[3] When they realize that is not always the case, they tend to blame uncomprehending foreigners either for their malice or for their short-sightedness in not seeing that French policies serve both the national interest and the broader interests of regional and world stability.[4] This is especially so with regard to the United States.

All French students are taught that their country played a decisive role—ideologically as well as militarily—in the creation of the United States. On the topic of the American Revolution, no French schoolbook fails to laud the contributions of Lafayette, Rochambeau, and others to the

American struggle for independence.[5] Not surprisingly, this contribution is frequently amplified or glorified. The realization among French officials that France is frequently distinctly unpopular among their American counterparts comes as a shock and corroborates their view that Americans do not understand their external environment or appreciate the outlook and attitudes of others.

The French are inclined to seek guidance from history and to apply its lessons to present-day situations. The French political debate focuses on historical events.[6] The United States, by contrast, is a country that was "born against history," to use Octavio Paz's phrase. Its gaze is focused on the present. Furthermore, Americans' connection with their own national past is more abstract.[7] Historical figures whom few Americans would identify with France, such as Benjamin Franklin and Thomas Jefferson, are correctly identified by all educated French citizens as having been closely associated with France.[8] Because of their proclivity for using the past to make sense of the present, the French are inclined to exaggerate the effect of historical links on the actual state of French-American relations. The two nations' historical ties cut two ways. As much as most French people recognize the role played by the United States in the service of their freedom twice in the twentieth century, many remember more or less consciously the questionable attitude of the Roosevelt administration toward Charles de Gaulle and the Resistance movement. Washington's decision to establish the Allied Government in Occupied Territories (AMGOT) in liberated France, with instructions (wisely ignored by General Dwight Eisenhower) to imprison Free French prefects if they refused to cede authority, is an irksome memory.[9] Therefore, whereas Americans expect only gratitude on the part of the French for their heroics in both world wars, French feelings border on resentment that the United States often behaved high-handedly, a sentiment found even among those who are genuinely thankful for America's critical contribution to liberation and victory.

In many Americans' view, their "rescue" of France from potential defeat in 1917 and from occupation in 1944 has never elicited the effusive gratitude it deserves. France's prickly rejection of American tutelage and its occasional relish in playing the role of the spoiler are interpreted in Washington as gestures of frustrated national ambition. Prideful French nationalism evokes little comprehension or sympathy, and instead a good measure of disparagement, in American policy circles. From the standpoint of officials in Paris, the United States insists on displays of appreciation for actions

Uncle Sam has taken mainly in its own self-interest. Sentimentality cannot be manipulated to justify America's relegation of its allies to the status of junior partners obediently contributing to U.S.-led enterprises whose design and objectives have been set in Washington. It is always easy to remember those times when one's country pursued great causes in service to the larger world. Hence the French focus on the American war for independence while the Americans keep foremost in mind their twentieth-century military successes.[10]

The resilience of French-American ties is manifest in the way they have always remained together in emergencies.[11] De Gaulle unconditionally supported the United States during the Cuban missile crisis in October 1962 and was firmer than any other European leader during the second Berlin crisis a year earlier. Likewise, President François Mitterrand, in his address to the German Bundestag in 1983, forcefully made the case for implementing NATO's double-track decision to deploy intermediate nuclear forces (INF) on the territory of five European allies (though not in France) as a response to the positioning of SS-20s by the Soviet Union. As a Socialist lecturing the German Social Democrats opposed to new nuclear deployments, he played a pivotal role in bolstering German resolve in the face of a Soviet propaganda campaign aimed at Germany's pacifist-oriented public opinion.[12] Thus France has been a reliable ally of the United States in times of crisis, even if it has played the role of the maverick at other times—behavior that many American officials resented as a complicating factor in managing the complexities of a multinational alliance.

Today, in the relatively placid post–cold war era, the French point of view has to be reckoned with above all because of its influence on the developing European Union. European construction owes much to French ideas, to French diplomacy, and to French officials in key positions within the EU Commission. The names of Jean Monnet, Robert Schuman, and, in a different sense, Charles de Gaulle spring to mind when one considers the founding of the European Community and the Franco-German reconciliation that cemented it. As president of the EU Commission, Jacques Delors charted the community's dramatic renewal after 1989. The EU as we now know it is inconceivable without an appreciation of why and how much France has influenced its form. Many of its structures and standard operating procedures seem to come directly from a textbook on French administrative science. Monetary union, the Common Foreign and Security Policy (CFSP), and the ambitious European Security and Defense Policy (ESDP) are enterprises that were spawned in Paris.

The European Vision

It was in historical character for France to be the one Western power to challenge outright both the ideological message and the political domination of the United States. The emergence of a Europe that transcended the artificial cold war divide was in accord with the French reading of history. De Gaulle's phrase "Europe de l'Atlantique à l'Oural" seemed to have been premonitory, as French leaders were quick to point out. The soon-to-be-adopted American slogan "from Vancouver to Vladivostok" was viewed as a sort of homage to the foresighted French leader, albeit misconceived in its political geography. The most compelling question for the French government in this new setting was how to maintain the influence it exerted in Western Europe during the cold war. American references to a "partnership in leadership" with Germany was a particular cause of dismay. It aroused fears in French minds of German-American collusion in managing the new Europe. That would mean an end to the crucial French-German relationship that had been the bedrock of France's position in Europe since the 1950s. The strenuous effort by French policymakers in the early 1990s to enlist Bonn in a strategy of expanding the powers of the European Union, thereby preparing it to be the predominant influence on continental affairs, was a reaction to the perceived threat presented by America's continued prominence in Europe.

In fact, the decision by the United States to anchor its European policy on a reunited Germany was not meant to undermine French influence, even if Washington was habitually impatient with France's contrarian voice. Rather, it was a pragmatic recognition that with unification the weight of Germany was increasing while the utility of the cold war instruments of leverage over German policy was weakening. New bonds had to be forged. Moreover, the Federal Republic of Germany had nurtured countless links with the American foreign policy community and had come to enjoy a trust among American elites as a government and a country that could be relied on. France, by contrast, had not made the necessary effort to ensure that its conception of a rebalanced Euro-American relationship was well understood and that France's value as a partner in making it serve American as well as European interests was appreciated.

The future shape of Europe was the overriding question for a Washington rethinking its world role. Europe had been the cockpit of the cold war. Its strategic value was undiminished. In economic terms, Europe's industrial and financial strength was nearly on a par with that of the United

States. Geostrategically, it provided the United States with an impregnable base of operations for projecting military force into other regions and with a partner for influencing political development in Central and Eastern Europe. The European allies also could contribute to dealing with threats to Western interests outside Europe, such as in the Gulf, where the fraught situation associated with the reflagging of Kuwaiti oil tankers in 1987–88 was a forerunner to the graver crisis provoked by the Iraqi invasion in 1990. Moreover, natural affinities of culture, history, and political values made the United States' status as a European power seem natural—a perception shared to differing degrees by most European capitals, if only with rueful qualification in Paris. A tight weave of institutional ties had created an implicit Euro-American web whose continued existence the United States saw as a prerequisite for success in the historic enterprise of extending the West's beneficent reach across Europe to embrace the former communist lands—eventually including Russia.

The challenge for American policymakers was to establish terms for the transatlantic partnership consonant with the American stake in Europe's welfare and with Europe's continued reliance on the United States' reassuring presence and at the same time to advance their mutual interest in fashioning a more egalitarian partnership. Achieving the last would prove most daunting. The West's victory in the cold war highlighted the discrepancies inherent in the Euro-American alliance. As long as American guardianship protected Western Europe from Soviet communism, it was experienced as natural and necessary.

The administrations of Presidents George H. W. Bush and Bill Clinton believed that the intangible assets that only the United States could bring to a collective Western strategy were enough to justify their retaining a leadership role in ordering the political space of post–cold war Europe. Unmatched American prestige, credibility, and political authority were indisputable facts of transatlantic life. Moreover, as a nation derivative of Europe yet detached from its troubled historical inheritance, the United States held a unique position. Indeed, for many Europeans, America was a kindred country, if disengaged from the passions that have left an indelible mark on political consciousness across the continent.

France rejected this proprietary view of the United States. French acquiescence in the American protection during the cold war had followed the dictates of an inescapable realism. This dependency nonetheless offended national pride: it compromised the French sense of nationhood, and it contradicted the principle of self-reliance embedded in a realist conception of international politics. Thus it was wholly predictable that in the self-scrutiny induced by the cold war's end those features of the preexisting transatlantic partnership most congenial to Washington should be viewed as unnatural and outdated by Paris.

France stood out from most of its Western European partners in finding the prospect of playing a role on the wider global stage inviting. It could reasonably aspire to augment its influence in places where it had historical ties and traditionally was involved. To extend its sights farther afield, though, it would have to convince other Western European governments that they had reason and means to do more than follow placidly in the United States' wake on those occasions when they ventured beyond their home waters.

The transatlantic strategic partnership, as viewed from Paris, served a utilitarian purpose. However facilitated by shared values, it remained no more than a practical arrangement among sovereign states—an arrangement of diminishing utility. France derived its international identity from its own distinctive traditions and status in the world, now supplemented by the truly transnational community that it formed with fellow members of the EU. It could not be content as a subordinate member of an American-led Western alliance. Accordingly, France would challenge continuation of the United States' primacy in European affairs along with the American claim to a *droit de regard* in selecting which issues to take charge of.

France welcomed the cold war's end as much for the return to "normalcy" as for the heralded victory for the liberal democracies that it undeniably was. Paris, more than other Western capitals, had found life under the American military umbrella vexing.[13] Throughout the cold war the French chafed at Americans' presumption in claiming to speak and act for a supposedly single-minded Western alliance, rejected outright Washington's claim to superior wisdom and moral conscience, and never ceased to be discomfited by their relegation to a secondary role in East-West diplomacy. Indeed, in the de Gaulle era, France pursued its own version of détente, predating Washington's, based on a belief in the mutability of the Soviet system and the durability of Russian national identity that sooner or later would erode the East-West division of Europe.[14] De Gaulle's seeming compulsion to assert France's exceptionality in self-conscious displays of independence from the United States was interpreted in American policy circles as contrariness for its own sake. Most Americans did not recognize the larger meaning of Gaullism as the expression of France's deeply felt belief in an identity and a calling that could not be subsumed within some nebulous entity, the West, under U.S. tutelage. That belief also complicated life for the United States as an alliance leader and made some uncomfortable because it resembled America's own self-image. Gaullism, as sentiment and as strategic concept, was nonetheless the genuine expression of views that have permeated the French body politic. As Philip Gordon has written, "A national strategic culture with deep roots in history and geography is not easily abandoned."[15]

That culture is suffused with an abiding sense of France's exceptionality. Together, its past grandeur, its distinctive and cultivated *mode de vie*, and its sense of destiny to illuminate and to instruct form an exalted self-image. It follows that "France should have an independent point of view on all the great problems of the planet with the ambition to play a role in their management."[16]

The successive French governments held steadfastly to this view of their singular place in the world throughout the long years of the cold war, where it survived as a minor theme in a grand drama whose starring roles were played by others. They could hardly be expected to abandon it at the very moment when conditions had become favorable once again to enunciate it. President François Mitterrand gave the sense of liberating most of France's foreign policy elite. For him, the events of 1989 punctuated the end of a prolonged interregnum: "Europe, yesterday dependent on the two superpowers, now, like one going home will go back to its history and geography."[17] (An American official, hearing these remarks, was heard to mutter: "God forbid.") Mitterrand had a deep and nostalgic historical memory that pervaded his thoughts even as he sought to come to terms with a world metamorphosing before his eyes. As his senior foreign affairs adviser and later chief of staff of the presidential office, Hubert Védrine, has commented: "The lessons of history were for him present on a daily basis, an almost obsessive presence."[18] Not surprisingly, Mitterrand instinctively sought intellectual coherence in a vision of Europe's future that downplayed the anomalous feature represented by the United States' cold war predominance.

The United States still had a valued place in Europe. However, it was America's symbolic presence that counted most. American troops were the tangible expression of that presence; NATO, the organizational vehicle for their deployment. Both were welcome, in modified form. An institutionalized American presence served a number of salutary purposes: anchoring Germany to the West and thereby countering any tendency it might have to shift its geostrategic outlook eastward; reassuring the skittish Eastern Europeans; and discouraging the renationalization of defense structures and policies. Moreover, NATO's multilateral structure—exemplified by the unanimity rule for the initiation of military action—imposed a measure of constraint on the United States' unilateralist impulse. These virtues led to the conclusion that "the defense of Western Europe, for the present and for many years to come, can only be conceived of in a context of respect for the Atlantic alliance . . . [which] will continue fully to play its major role in the maintenance of peace," as President Mitterrand averred in April 1991.[19]

Avowed strategic considerations mixed with apprehensions about insular trends in the United States. They dated from the mid-1980s when the early signs of revived neo-isolationist sentiment along with growing financial strains and a lengthening list of social problems evoked fears of a progressive disengagement from Europe. The French wondered whether these trends might be accelerated now that the United States had lost a compelling strategic justification to remain.

Paris thus faced a double challenge: to calibrate how much of a continued American involvement made sense for France; and to settle on a policy line that struck the right balance in developing European community institutions, including the building of a security and defense capability, without thereby adding to the ebb tide pulling the United States away from European shores. The preferred transatlantic relationship would be a better balanced one in which France would accept a certain American influence in Europe in order to similarly influence American policy, all the while benefiting from the United States' sedative effect on continental politics. Shaping a set of arrangements to accommodate the United States on French terms was far more trying than setting the objective. In striving to do so, France had to contend with its other great concern: a unified Germany. Bonn, like Paris, had regained a measure of strategic free will. France's two critical relationships called for different forms of adjustment. While Paris sought to revise the terms of dependency on the United States, it sought simultaneously to maintain the terms of a partnership with Bonn that enhanced French influence while inhibiting German power. Much ingenuity was devoted to finding a formula that accomplished that double purpose.

The simplest course might have been for France to overcome its qualms about perpetuating NATO's dominance in European security, reclaim its full place in the alliance, and thereby ensure that the Atlantic alliance would continue to curb any wayward tendencies that Germany might develop. This hope, entertained in Washington, was short lived. The French government under François Mitterrand did not abandon its deep reservations about an unreformed U.S.-led NATO dominating European affairs in order to constrain Germany. A deepened European Community, as elaborated in the blueprint provided by the Maastricht Treaty on European Union, with its emphasis on economic and monetary union among the existing EU members, was visualized as the primary instrument for doing so. France's opting for "Europe" as its answer to the German question reflected both the confidence in its ability to keep its leverage on the Federal Republic and the risks it was prepared to run to resist a renewed American hegemony.

French and German interests converged in pointing toward a bold step in European construction. They were not identical, though; nor did Paris and Bonn share the same expectations in building Europe. Germany was willing, in theory, to merge its national identity with a European entity. France was not. Sensitive to its neighbors' uneasiness about the strength of a reunited Germany, the government of German chancellor Helmut Kohl pursued the grandly self-effacing strategy of providing reassurance in all directions. It had a compelling reason to expand the authority of the EU's institutions in Brussels and found congenial the transfer of powers to a supranational body. France, in contrast, had little inclination to sublimate its national personality. The unification of Europe as an end in itself appealed to only a thin stratum of the French political elite and resonated far less positively among the French public than it did across the Rhine. Accordingly, in Paris's vision of an enhanced European community, inter-governmental cooperation, centered on the European Council (of heads of state and government) and on the European Council of Ministers, figured as prominently as did empowering the supranational European Commission. This was especially true for the French plans for a Common Foreign and Security Policy. The challenge for France was to promote full integration in spheres that would attenuate German power—such as monetary union—while resisting the push toward political union elsewhere.[20]

The Mitterrand government was confident it could do so. The ambitious Maastricht plan for community construction, extending into the field of defense and foreign policy, was the centerpiece of an audacious French strategy designed to reconfirm the EC as the core of an emerging European system, restrict American influence, magnify French influence, and prepare the ground for "Europe" to become a player on the world stage. France believed that it could remain the EC's guiding spirit, its deft diplomacy making the community into an enlarged conception of itself. Chancellor Kohl's conviction that dramatic measures were called for to bind Germany more tightly to multilateral institutions, thereby inoculating itself against the temptations of nationalism, gave France the irresistible opportunity to raise its sights. A qualitative expansion of the European Community's powers, including a transfer to a European Central Bank of the prerogatives of the Deutsche Bundesbank, would raise the odds against a rekindling of German national ambition. At the same time, it offered the prospect that Western Europe would marshal its collective resources to form a new hub of power, one capable of managing the continent's affairs and projecting influence beyond Europe's borders. Instead of a unitary West under American direction, French officials boldly pictured a contrasting image of a partnership between two entities that shared the same core interests and values but remained politically distinct.

Achieving this vision of Europe simultaneously would enable France to assert its national genius and to promote continental stability. In François Mitterrand's optimistic phrasing: "France will be all the more influential, prosperous, and radiant in the world if she plays her role in Europe, and this role will be consistent with her history, a determining role."[21] The paradoxical element in this formulation was captured by the ironic comment of Daniel Vernet that "for France to remain France, it must become European."[22]

The French push to build "Europe" was linked to a broader design for a re-equilibrated continent. A self-reliant Western Europe would be the firm mooring for a pan-European confederation embracing the former communist lands. It was conceived as a loose association—including Russia but excluding the United States—to restore a sense of sharing a common political and cultural space throughout Europe. Envisioned as encompassing a range of elements from collective security to the promotion of economic links, the ill-starred confederation project, a prized personal scheme of President Mitterrand, never took off.[23] It was resented in the East as second-quality goods fobbed off by its self-absorbed Western cousins and as a structure that ran the danger of being dominated by the still-existing Soviet Union. Washington for its part made disapproving noises about an organization that would exclude the United States. Mitterrand, though, placed blame for the plan's ignominious collapse at the doorstep of Germany. Bonn's coolness toward the confederation idea was interpreted as an indication of a German ambition to reserve most of Eastern Europe for itself as an area for German economic and cultural penetration. The Bush administration mistakenly thought that it was being judged the culprit. The three sides of the Washington-Paris-Bonn triangle in fact were connected insofar as the Kohl government was leery of any architectonic plans for post–cold war Europe that excluded the United States. France's two obsessions had become tangled in a way that American policymakers could not fully comprehend, especially since in characteristic fashion the French were free with their public criticisms of the United States while remaining discreet when it came to discontent with Germany.

By "Europeanizing" much of its foreign policy, France has constrained its definition and execution. France is associated with publicly declared EU positions that run against the grain of American policy, including the ban on antipersonnel land mines, the agreements of the Rio Convention on biodiversity, the establishment of the International Criminal Court, and the status of Palestine. All of these bones of contention with the United States attest to French diplomatic activism that is dedicated to constituting Europe as a force on the world stage. They also reveal how France has been forced to accommodate itself to prevailing sentiment among other European countries. The strengthening and institutionalization of international law has not always been a traditional French instinct. It has become so as France simultaneously integrates its policies with EU partners and perceives an advantage in building rule-based international regimes. France has become susceptible to what Robert Cooper calls "the post-modern foreign policy syndrome."[24] The increasing Europeanization of France's foreign policy has blurred the line between France's own thinking and that influenced by its partners. This element of ambiguity makes it easier in one sense and more difficult in another to place French-American relations on a surer footing. Bilateral dealings are less stark. They are partly diffused in wider U.S.-EU exchanges. The stakes, though, are high and growing. Moreover, the laborious processes of consensus building within the EU render any agreed position resistant to modification. The resulting inflexibility, as evident in the tense trade negotiations between the United States and the European Union, is usually blamed on French machinations. That is true in large part because France characteristically voices European positions more squarely—though not more confrontationally—than do its partners. The handling of the trade disputes over bananas, hormone additives in beef, and genetically engineered foodstuffs are cases in point. The EU's demand for a place in the Israeli-Palestinian peace process is another. Policies that emerge from a broad European consensus all too often get stigmatized and dismissed in Washington as French-inspired protection of crass self-interest.

Europeanization of French foreign policy has quite another implication. Since the United States is trusted more in most other European countries than in France, French diplomacy has been obliged to take the American factor more fully into account in defining Europe as a political project, a condition implicitly demanded by France's European partners—hence the French rapprochement with NATO in 1995–97, a more relaxed French attitude starting in 1994 concerning NATO's direction of peace-keeping operations in the Balkans,[25] and Paris's acquiescence in arrangements that circumscribe the independence of ESDP planning structures. France's adaptation to EU circumstances is all the more remarkable given the acute sense of national history and exalted self-image that pervade the French political consciousness. The net effect is that in any given case one cannot readily disentangle what is of purely French inspiration and what is due to the need for achieving a unified EU position. That state of affairs disconcerts the French and confuses Americans. Washington officials find the lengthy and convoluted European Union processes for reaching decisions vexing. Delay in making up its collective mind is matched by the exceptional difficulty of altering common positions that have been so arduously attained. An impression of stubbornness and inflexibility is created, an impression with a French coloration. EU policies indeed frequently are disproportionately influenced by Paris. When at odds with American policy, the collective strength of the EU makes it harder for the United States to get its way—an aggravation of French-American relations following in its train. In this way, the string of contentious trade disputes that have bedeviled transatlantic relations are exacerbated by the French factor.

France's Multipolar Perspective

From a global perspective, France's strategic conception contrasts a healthy multipolarity with American hegemony. *Multipolarity* is a recurrent motif in French discourse about international affairs, one that acquired new accent with Jacques Chirac's arrival at the Elysée Palace. The frequent reference to multipolarity in declarations by French leaders, however, raises more questions than it answers. Is it just a revival of an instinctive Gaullism rebelling against American domination of European affairs and self-assertive nationalism now given global breadth? Does it mean a return to the classic game of power balancing? If so, what are the interests in conflict between the United States and France that dictate balancing rather than acting in concert? If the perception is of mixed convergent and divergent interests, then what is the right formulation for reconciling the two? If Europe is to be the entity that countervails American power, what does that imply for maintaining France's rank as a world power?

There are no easy or right answers to these questions. France's predisposition to resist what it sees as the danger of American hegemony arises from the belief that power relationships are the essence of international affairs. Hence, U.S. power must be checked lest it lead to an unhealthful unilateralism—involving the imposition of its ideas and its will—unalloyed by the thoughts and participation of others. It is reinforced by prideful confidence that France as a nation has a calling to make its voice heard, unstifled by an overbearing United States. French emphasis on opposing what it interprets as implicit American claims to dominion prompts some Americans to the facile conclusion that France contests the U.S. position and power instinctively. This interpretation distorts a more complex reality of what shapes French thinking and animates its foreign policy. France is not dedicated to reviving the classic game of *raison d'état*.

French foreign policy can properly be called revisionist in another respect. It would alter the distribution of power among the Western democracies, in their own multilateral institutions and in comprehensive international organizations (the United Nations [UN] and the International Monetary Fund [IMF]), as well as in dealings with third parties. In order to do so, Europe (that is, the EU) must acquire the requisite means and aptitude. That entails a double transformation: perfecting mechanisms for coordinating and sustaining policies toward the rest of the world and adding a security dimension to the EU's "civilian" power. In President Chirac's words, "In endowing itself with a capacity for military action, [Europe] becomes a complete political actor."[26] However, France's goal of building a political influence commensurate with the EU's economic prowess has not been shared fully by most other EU governments. Still, in the economic realm, the European Commission has won the permission of national governments to represent its collective interest in international negotiations on commercial and financial matters. Consequently, the EU has an influence commensurate with its size in engineering modifications and extensions of the global trade regime centered around the World Trade Organization (WTO). Similarly, the euro is destined to become an international transaction and reserve currency on a par with the dollar, its early weakness notwithstanding. Europe's stake in the working of multilateral institutions will rise accordingly.

That evolution is a natural extension of the EU's success in integrating Western European economies. The obligation to deal with the international issues it engenders conforms with the type of benevolent technocratic management that Brussels has come to exercise in what is widely perceived as the virtuous cause of enhancing the well-being of community citizens. Foreign and defense policy are quite another matter. Not only does the EU have little experience and no proven record of accomplishment, but its methods are at variance with standard operating procedures in the security sphere. Confrontation, coercion, and conflict—staples of foreign policy— are viewed as unsavory but not illegitimate by large segments of opinion in many EU countries. The community's most notable foray into the thicket of conflict management—in the former Yugoslavia in 1992–95—was a conspicuous and embarrassing failure, exacerbated by unguarded American criticism from the outside.

French policymakers have been very much aware of these inhibitions. Mounting a campaign to ready Europe to contend with American hegemonic power has consumed a heavy share of French diplomatic energy. It is justified as a way of giving Europe, and indirectly France, a status equal to that of the United States. The resulting challenge to American domination in the 1990s was a clear rejection of the single-superpower model of the post–cold war international system. Less clear is whether that challenge is made on behalf of a traditional multipolar model (with an assumption of contradictory interests and rivalry among those holding the polar positions). It is rather best understood as based on the idea of a loosely constructed dominant pole composed of the liberal democracies that is distinguishable from other, weaker poles or hubs. Those other hubs (Russia, China, India) should be recognized as sovereign players with their own legitimate interests that have to be taken into account even as a patient Western diplomacy seeks to mute differences and encourages them to take the path of democracy and enlightened external relations. Such a conception would allow Western countries to pursue somewhat different policies toward other states, and even vie for preferential economic and political ties with them. It also would allow for promotion of different plans and designs for institutionalizing the multilateral principle—whether in the UN Security Council, the International Monetary Fund, or the reform of NATO. That could occur without calling into question the underlying comity of fundamental interests among the Western democracies. After all, France does not see the United States as a foe in a deadly struggle of power politics. It does not deny the sharing of strategic interests. Paris accepts, too, that those interests should be expressed in wider multinational bodies, such as the UN—even as tactical differences may arise on individual issues.

The value of multilateral cooperation generally has risen as France's traditional adherence to a *raison d'état* doctrine has loosened its grip on the minds of foreign policymakers. National rivalry is still seen as the norm but as highly variable in time and circumstance. The corollary is that cooperation among states is not perceived merely as a temporary suspension of natural patterns. France certainly believed that the EC institutions it had done so much to construct to last would outlive the cold war's end. It also had come to see a measure of truth in liberal institutionalism, broadly speaking. The organizations created to handle the affairs of the Western democracies are valued for their utility and for ordering relations among the compatible industrial democracies. At the global level, the contribution of multilateral economic bodies, above all the International Monetary Fund and the General Agreement on Tariffs and Trade (GATT)/World Trade Organization, to economic stability and growth is readily acknowledged—even as skepticism is registered about the more optimistic claims of those (largely Americans) who see the spread of market capitalism as the foundation for a world edifice of peace.

It is true that French foreign policy elites welcomed the *renaissance de stratégie* that the passing of the cold war permitted. A reversion to the *jeu des nations* in the full, traditional meaning of the term was neither expected nor desired, however. The strong realist streak in the French outlook is not to be confused with the bleak—and misguided—pessimism of John Mearsheimer's "back to the future."[27] More pertinent is whether the French intellectual comfort in contemplating the *jeu des nations* too easily justified its zeal to weaken the United States' hold on European affairs and its claims of *droit de regard* elsewhere. It leads some Americans to conclude that France instinctively plays the game for the game's sake. That is to say, France is accused of seeking status enhancement per se, appraising collective enterprises according to the French imprint on their design as much as their accomplishment of avowed purposes. This interpretation is a distortion of what actually shapes French thinking and animates its diplomacy. In today's world, the objective of a responsible French foreign policy is to curb the excesses of American power, to resist its hegemonic impulse, and to promote a healthy multilateralism.

Where collective interests are at issue, then Washington's preponderant influence means that American preferences are most likely to dictate the course taken. In Paris's eyes, they are as likely as not to be misguided, no better than policies and plans advocated by others. The United States' primacy

in multilateral institutions biases how they reach decisions and their substance. In the case of the IMF, votes are weighted using a formula that gives
Washington a de facto veto over crucial decisions. In NATO, the criticality
of the United States as the alliance's linchpin ensures that U.S. views are
accorded exceptional respect: they define the problem, structure the
debate, and exercise disproportionate influence on the choices made. The
French are sensitive to the fact that NATO is intrinsically a military organization, hierarchically organized, which ensures a pervasive American
influence. Within the alliance, and in Western forums generally, the combination of American power and self-righteousness produces domineering
behavior. Consequently, in Hubert Védrine's words, the United States'
"weight carries them toward hegemonism, and the idea they have of their
mission is unilateralist."[28]

America's disproportionate influence places its partners at a disadvantage in the shaping of common policies—whether in the Balkans, in the
Middle East, or on IMF reform. French officials reject the implicit claim that
Uncle Sam knows best. Whether the issue is dealing with Saddam Hussein,
bringing Iran into the community of responsible nations, achieving a Pal-
estinian settlement, handling China's emergence as a great power, or bringing peace to Kosovo, American officials claim that their policies have greater
validity than what France advocates (and, on these issues, what many other
Europeans advocate). Irritation is particularly acute in Paris when Washington declares as its privileged domain disputes that touch Europe more
immediately than the United States. France for years has felt shut out of the
Israeli-Palestinian mediation; its views on recasting a strategy for containing
Iraq are ignored. Yet French—and European—stakes in each instance are as
great as, if not greater than, those of the United States. Europe is also mani-
festly more directly vulnerable to the consequences of errant American
policy—illegal migration, disrupted access to oil supplies, and, before
September 11, 2001, terrorism. The readiness of the George W. Bush administration to accept the EU as a partner in a renewed effort to break the
spiral of violence between Israelis and Palestinians has gone some distance
toward satisfying the French desire to be diplomatically engaged. Similarly,
Washington's recognition that there was some merit to French views on
alternatives to the unraveling sanctions regime imposed on Iraq was a welcome change. The preachy tone that can creep into the public utterances of
some senior American policymakers adds to the resentment at perceived
American high-handedness. The manner by which the United States exer-

cises its unmatched power as much as its control over outcomes grates on French sensibilities. Why is this more so in Paris than in other allied capitals?

One reason is that France at the beginning of the 1990s saw itself more as a direct rival of the United States—whether in shaping European security arrangements, in deciding on the appropriate approach to regulating international financial markets, or in the images and models of popular culture propagated around the world. In strictly commercial terms, French companies are no more competitors of American businesses than those of Germany or Britain. In most spheres, there is little that is exceptional about the rivalry. The difference is that France measures itself against the United States. The French-American rivalry is perceived as an encompassing one. That in itself lends importance to any aspect of it, at least for the French. Moreover, only France believes in the universal validity of its social and economic philosophy, its ideas, its culture, and therefore its aspirations to be one of a handful of nations whose voice deserves to be heard and whose opinion ought to count. Unsure of the rank others accord it, France traditionally has harbored few doubts that its ideas, institutions, and culture are world class. French leaders are conscious that their country was the cradle of the Enlightenment and the Declaration of the Rights of Man, a living truth that carries with it a presumption to act within a magisterial moral universe. This belief is indeed matched by no other nation except, of course, America. More often than not, it is the global dominance of the United States that eclipses French accomplishments and blocks France from assuming its rightful place in the sun. Universalism is not an easy thing to share.

France is as keen to attenuate what it sees as overweening American influence on a global scale as it is eager to construct an omnicompetent EU that will enable the Europeans to be masters of their own affairs. In Paris's critique of the single-superpower model, the value of other self-willed actors playing larger parts figures prominently—thus its activism in developing a regular discourse between the EU and Asian powers, including a structured dialogue with its counterpart in the Association of Southeast Asian Nations (ASEAN). Against this backdrop, it is easier to discern the meaning attached to President Chirac's signing, in 1997, of a joint communiqué in Beijing with Chinese president Jiang Zemin that pledged the two countries "to engage in reinforced cooperation, to foster the march toward multipolarity . . . and to oppose any attempt at domination in world affairs."[29] The response of U.S. officials to this veiled reference to alleged American hegemonic impulses mixed dismay with incomprehension. The official underreaction to being so stigmatized by a close ally owed more to weary acceptance of the inevitable French rhetoric than it did to an appreciation of the nuanced thinking that lay behind it.

Ironically, France's continuing preoccupation with the United States coincides with the current of self-doubt that has crept into France's ongoing discourse about itself. Belief in French singularity and mission now coexists with a contrary element of introverted self-criticism. That recurring phenomenon in French society tends to discover a fresh national malaise on an almost cyclical basis. Ambition and morosity contest each other within the collective French consciousness. One recent bout of introspective scrutiny sprang from domestic troubles: the long string of tawdry political corruption scandals. It also is fed by frustration in the country's external relations. The shifting of weight in the French-German partnership is proving difficult to accept and to handle. Further afield, the reversion from its long-standing role of gendarme and patron in the francophone community of sub-Saharan states is the most striking manifestation of this attitude. The calling into question of what has amounted to a modern-day *mission civilisatrice* was catalyzed by the tragedy in Rwanda in the 1990s. French material and political support for the Hutu-led government that instigated the genocide induced qualms about the moral justification for a policy of paternalism (even if official inquiries absolved the French government of any responsibility). The rethinking in Paris of its African engagements, in its early phase, was laced with recrimination about heavy-handed American attempts to build U.S. influence in the region at French expense. The United States' backing for anglophone political forces contesting with francophone rivals in the Congo and the adjacent Great Lakes region added a combustible linguistic element to the mix. The subsequent compromise arrangements reached by Paris and Washington over Africa owes something to France's reassessment of its stake in Africa as well as in the wider context of growing French-American cordiality.

The Globalization Issue

France's national soul-searching notwithstanding, it remains a country that has an exalted sense of self and that takes easy offense. At moments of acute stress between Washington and Paris, French officials and diplomats seem especially haunted by the specter of an omnipresent and potent American influence—whether emanating from the Pentagon and the State Department or Hollywood—that dominates an emerging global society. Globalization looks indistinguishable from Americanization of the planet, an assault on both France's standing and its cultural integrity. For those who see the nation's *mode de vie* imperiled, cultural imperialism could seem a grave threat to France's identity and integrity.

In a more practical vein, globalization erodes the ability of the state to protect its citizens against the vagaries of markets and against those who use the markets to purvey their commercial practices and influence in ways that may be antithetical to French traditions and economic well-being. The French state, which for hundreds of years has provided order and security, no longer can impose its will on the means and ends of that historic commitment. The tools forged over generations to serve the nation have lost their fine edge. For the French nation to avoid dissolving in the "magma" of an amorphous anglophone international society (to use an expression of Hubert Védrine), to maintain control over its own fate, and to fulfill its obligations to the collective good, the French welfare state must innovate where possible and accommodate where necessary, while preserving, whenever it can, what is of proven value.[30] The dialectic between attachment to the tried and tested recipes and the impulse to confront and master what is new and challenging creates a constant tension in France's encounters with the contemporary world. It has little prospect of yielding a stable synthesis.

France's promotion of a multipolar international system combines a diagnosis of what it believes are the two key sources of instability with a set of prescriptions for putting them under the collective control of responsible political authority. Globalization is the overriding reality of our times. Embodied in the integrated world markets, cross-national business networks, and unbounded communication networks, it carries as much risk as it does promise. The power of an open world economy to generate wealth is unprecedented. So, too, is its potential, when inadequately regulated, to disrupt healthy commercial and financial interchanges. This is particularly true of capital and currency markets, which function in a transnational space beyond the reach of national governments and multilateral organizations. The financial panics of 1997–98 exemplify how rapidly shocks can be transmitted from one region to another. The societies of Western Europe and North America are not immune to these virulent epidemics, either in their economic repercussions or in their political effects. Political upheaval resulting from economic trauma in Russia or East Asia jeopardizes Europe's stake in a progressive and orderly world system.

The United States bears a share of the responsibility for this troubled state of affairs. As the fountainhead of orthodox liberal doctrines, it has used its immense prestige to propagate its conception of a harmonious world system. From the French vantage point, the United States has conjured up an illusory vision "of a more homogeneous world, rationalized and pacified by the end of the cold war, of the generalization of the Western liberal model," in Foreign Minister Hubert Védrine's words. "This illusion is now dissipated. We are neither at the end of history, nor [do we] inhabit the magical New World order."[31]

A sharp critique of Washington's assiduous campaign in favor of a dogmatic free-market doctrine takes strength from the conviction that the underlying philosophy is both misguided and used to mask a strategy of creating advantageous opportunities for American business—whether in financial services, communications, or entertainment. The United States' push for Asian countries to open their capital markets prematurely is seen as a major cause of the financial crisis that has ravaged the region. Moreover, the disruptive consequences were aggravated and prolonged by the International Monetary Fund's mishandling of the crisis, which is ascribed to the undue influence of American doctrine on the IMF's lending policies and the crucial American role in designing the fund's rescue plans.

Similarly, the 1998 collapse of financial markets in Russia is interpreted as due in good measure to its following a course laid out by "ultraliberal dogmatism."[32] Russia's plight, which jeopardizes the historic project of assimilating it into a comprehensive European system, was the result of an ill-considered experiment with "ultraliberal" gimmicks—promoted by American advisers and applied with callous disregard for the absence of essential state structures—which doomed it to a failure with profound social and political consequences. By placing the blame for the adverse turn in Russia's fortunes on the doorstep of the United States, French officials vividly illustrate what they see as the liabilities of America's ideological as well as power-political dominance in the great enterprises of the post–cold war world.

The spotlight focused on globalization by the antiglobalization demonstrations at the G-8 economic summit in Genoa in July 2001 spurred French leaders to forcefully articulate their own outlook, one that stands in opposition to the outspoken faith of the Bush administration in the power of markets to work good in the world. Both Jacques Chirac and Lionel Jospin expressed their aversion to untrammeled market forces whose capacity for wealth creation can also be accompanied by dislocation and deprivation. Jospin proclaimed that France rejoices in "the worldwide emergence of a citizens' movement [that] expresses the wish of a majority of mankind better to share the potential fruits of globalization." In his view, a process of globalization that is "badly managed" and "leads to a widening gap in inequality" calls for "putting into place regulatory mechanisms at the international level, which implies a new role for states."[33] Speaking in a more moderate vein, President Chirac declared, "Our democracies, clearly, cannot be mere spectators of globalization. They must tame it, accompany it, humanize it, civilize it."[34]

American hegemony figures alongside globalization as the second source of instability in this anxious assessment. The United States is depicted by Védrine as a "hyperpower"—that is to say, "a power without precedent since Roman times, dominant in every field: military, technological, monetary, fashion, culture."[35] As he has stated, "We cannot accept either a world politically unipolar or a world culturally uniform, or the unilateralism of the sole hyperpower. That is why we are fighting for a world that is multipolar, diversified, and multilateral."[36]

Védrine's repeated references to the United States as a "hyperpower" have grated on the ears of members of Congress who base their understanding of the term on misleading press accounts. Observer Christopher Caldwell has even coined the term "Védrinism" to stigmatize a supposedly revisionist French tendency.[37] Although in English the prefix "hyper-" can mean "excessive," in French it refers neither to hype nor to anything derogatory. It simply means "larger than super." Very large French supermarkets are known as *hypermarchés*. The minister's insistence on using an expression that he now knows offends American ears is partly author's pride, but also perhaps an expression of disbelief that his phrase could be thus misinterpreted. To Americans, it seems to be saying that is for them to adapt to French concepts. Whereas American statesmen understand how far France has moved in adapting itself to the durability and naturalness of U.S. power, the intellectual formulations French officials use to explain their government's thinking are too readily misinterpreted. In public diplomacy, and virtually all U.S. diplomacy today is done in public, simplicity has its virtues.

These French and American preconceptions are unhelpful on several counts. For one thing, the American propensity to take charge of everything, everywhere, to impose its views on every issue—from chastising Saddam Hussein to arranging bailouts for Brazil—makes problem solving hostage to the imperfect judgment and subjectivity of one country. With overweening power comes hubris, no matter how well-intentioned those who wield it may be. Unbalanced and unrestrained, a fallible America convinced of its rightness is prone to act unilaterally. That increases the likelihood of misguided or erroneous actions—such as being too quick to strike Iraq, imposing sanctions on products from the EU without waiting for the WTO dispute panel's ruling in the "banana war," or deploying a national missile defense without full prior consultation with allies and a sober reflection on how it could undermine the laboriously constructed system for maintaining nuclear stability. Unilateralism carries the further cost that the rules of a multilateral process and the principle of collective responsibility are slighted or ignored outright. The example set by the United States implicitly absolves other states of their obligation to act responsibly and weakens the norms of good international conduct. Furthermore, earnest debates tend to get short circuited, and honest differences get stifled. Thus France avowedly "strives for multilateral international relations to be based on clear principles of legality—to counteract U.S. dominance."[38] By legality, the French mean strict observance of international organizations' jurisdiction, their deliberative procedures, and their power to authorize action. It is a principle that French diplomacy is dedicated to upholding, whether in NATO councils, at the UN Security Council (UNSC), or within the policy-making machinery of the IMF. This also applies to informal forums such as the contact group, which has been prominent in the treatment of successive Balkan crises.

French strictures against self-appointed guardians of international security are obviously aimed at the United States. Paris makes no secret of its disquiet over the growing American propensity to judge and act unilaterally. The 1998 cruise missile attack in the Sudan and against Osama bin Laden's base in Afghanistan are among the most egregious examples. They, along with the spasmodic air assault on Iraq in December 1998, were viewed from Paris as evidence of a disturbing tendency to substitute high-tech military pyrotechnics for a well-considered strategy. Washington's seeming readiness to resort to economic sanctions as a coercive tool is another manifestation of impetuous unilateralism. Sanctions, too, should only be deployed with an enabling mandate from the UN Security Council, in the French view. Several considerations come together in this condemnation of the perceived American sanctions mania: a deep skepticism of their effectiveness, based on the historical record; anger at being the indirect target of the sanctions stipulated by the Helms-Burton and Kennedy-D'Amato Acts for commercial transactions with Iran, Libya, and Cuba; humanitarian concern over the suffering they can cause; and the belief that entrenching the principle of multilateralism serves to regularize and thereby pacify international relations—most especially in dispute resolution.

The observance of procedural norms is integral to France's plan for managing the rise of American power. A rule-based system helps to curb the excesses of American power that are otherwise unchecked by countervailing force. The United States, convinced of its superior judgment and prone to see its interests as identical to those of the international community, uncritically imposes its prescriptions for the world's ills unless forced to defend its views in a structured public forum. French leaders' repeated references to the United States as a hegemonic or hyperpower is, for them, a statement of fact. Rather than complain about it, they would prefer to deal with it in a way that minimizes detrimental effects while respecting the exceptional potential that the United States has for generating public goods.

The Erratic Partner

U.S. predominance becomes all the more detrimental to international stability as American policy is increasingly perceived as being erratic. The fading tradition of bipartisan foreign policy has fragmented the national consensus on the country's overseas engagements while opening the decisionmaking process to the vagaries of turbulent domestic politics. Paris finds it unnerving to "deal with a superpower at the head of which several policies contend with each other, contradict each other . . . [and] where there is a multiplication of mutually antagonistic decision centers."[39] The worst French fears of rampant partisanship and parochialism came true with the U.S. Senate's rejection of the Comprehensive Test Ban Treaty (CTBT) in October 1999. Unforeseen as well as potentially harmful to Western strategic interests, it shocked French leaders and the entire French political class. They could not reconcile the action with either Americans' image of themselves as the world's moral and political leader or the objective fact that the United States bears weighty responsibilities for upholding the rules and principles of an orderly world system. Inattentive to the signs of serious dissent from the strategic philosophy embodied in the CTBT, Paris saw only a "Congress too often ready to yield to the temptations of unilateralism and isolationism" and a White House unable to master it in the name of overriding international interests."[40] As observed from Paris, partisanship encroaching on foreign policy is particularly pronounced when an international issue touches a neuralgic point on the American body politic. The Helms-Burton and Kennedy-D'Amato Acts, which brought the United States and the European Union to the precipice before an expedient face-saving device was found and bedeviled transatlantic relations for two agonizing years, were initiatives of a willful, xenophobic Congress that a beleaguered White House lacked either the strength or the will to resist. The bitter constitutional confrontation created by President Clinton's affair with a White House intern and his subsequent impeachment shook all of America's allies, none more so than France with its extrasensitivity to the hazards of a rudderless superpower. There was more than courtesy expressed in President Chirac's phone call to Bill Clinton in September 1998 to remind him that "at a time when the world is faced with serious political and financial uncertainty, it is vital for all of us that the president of the United States is in a position to carry out his duties fully."[41] Chirac may have underestimated Clinton's powers of compartmentalization. But as the December 1998 air assault against Saddam Hussein and the White House's hesitancy over military action in Kosovo showed, the credibility of American diplomacy is unavoidably impaired when motivation and accountability are blurred by domestic turmoil.

For France to secure its interests in a world where the main dangers arise from a relentless process of globalization and the excessive power of an often maverick United States, it must find mechanisms for regulating the former and taming the latter. Rational policies and coherent strategies for executing them depend on achieving a measure of order and, thereby, predictability. The need to rely on improvisation to cope with turbulent markets or political crises in an unruly international system leaves French officials distinctly uneasy. However adept they may be at making adroit tactical adjustment to shifting conditions, improvisation is alien to their instinct for intellectual order and the deliberate action it makes possible. President Chirac expressed himself in this vein in his 1998 annual presidential address to the French ambassadorial corps, prefacing his remarks with this comment:

> This is the occasion for me to depict an international reality that is complex, sometimes irrational, in a Cartesian analysis. The need to affirm a global vision for the long term, instead of only dealing pragmatically with each issue as it arises, distinguishes our country, I believe. To analyze what one sees and to say what one wants is a necessary exercise for a great nation. The French need to know where they are going. And I have the feeling that in proposing its

vision for the twenty-first century our country will find itself
receiving wide assent in the world.[42]

There could be no truer summation of French philosophy, French
method, and French aspiration for managing its external relations. The cornerstone of the French project to regain a modicum of intellectual order,
which in turn is the basis for a coherent diplomatic strategy, is Europe.

The EU has been proclaimed an "empire of reason"—that is, a volun-
tary union of nations whose logical analysis of their interests led to a pool-
ing of sovereign powers. France's view of a unified Europe bears on its
assessment of French-American relations in two respects. The EU is conceived as a progressively integrating community whose supranational character endows it with a "legitimacy-producing" capacity that the more
loosely configured Atlantic community lacks.[43] Consequently, it will in the
long run win the allegiance of Western Europeans, thereby enabling it to act
in their name as an accountable power. In the French view, a new form of
sovereignty is being invented that unites sovereign nations so as "to recon-
quer a sovereignty that in fact has already vanished."[44] More fully empow-
ered EU institutions in Brussels could redeem the balance between state and
market, with the promise of greater predictability, stability, and manage-
ability of economic conditions. Similarly, they would bolster Western
Europe's capacity to influence external political developments via a Common Foreign and Security Policy. The latter judgment is based on two
premises: (1) that currently the European allies lack the clout to contend
with American power; and (2) that increasing resort to the EU as the instrument for promoting collective interests will not diminish the readiness of
publics to run risks and to accept sacrifices. Jacques Chirac, in promoting
the ESDP initiative, has said explicitly that the European Union should
"endow itself with all the instruments of a true power." It is only natural that
it should do so, he implies, because "now that they are reconciled among
themselves, Europeans yearn to assert themselves fully in the international
arena, to promote the values of humanism that are the wellspring of their
civilization, and to express a certain idea of man and society."[45] These echoes
of Charles de Gaulle in European garb are not surprising coming from a
Gaullist president.

If participating in a unified Europe is a crucial element in the French
plan for managing American hegemonic power, it is not a painless or cost-
free strategic course for France to take. To save itself from the dual threats of

unbridled globalization and American hegemonic influence, France must give up a part of its ability to act independently. That is the Faustian bargain Paris has made with the EU administration in Brussels. The struggle to reconcile the attachment to French particularity with the logic of community integration spurs the French government's efforts to bend collective policies to its will while raising the stakes on doing so successfully. The high profile of French ideas and French officials in the community lends a Gallic tinge to the EU, especially in American eyes. Contentious disputes over agriculture or cultural property (areas where French interests are prominent) reinforce the impression in the American media and Congress that French knee-jerk anti-Americanism lies behind recurrent quarrels on the trade front. Hence France's strategy for using the EU to counter American influence can aggravate already tense French-American and Euro-American relations.

Nonetheless, France remains dedicated to building up the EU as a major world power in its own right, not merely as a subset of an overarching Western community. The French notion that *l'Europe sera stratégique ou ne sera pas* (if Europe is to have a political existence, it must have a strategic personality) conveys the conviction that the goal of constituting the EU as a player on the world stage both validates and completes the project of European construction. A unified Europe is visualized as performing a critical stabilizing function by integrating and orchestrating the diverse voices of its constituent nations, because it can offset the weight of the United States and because it has the potential to assist and encourage the forces of democratic reform in the former communist lands to the east. A Europe "endowed with a project, an identity, and a capacity for international action is visualized as an essential building block for a better-balanced international system, one where cooperation among a number of hubs of power is more likely to be forthcoming and effective."[46] By acting in concert rather than individually, members of the European Union better position themselves to defend their interests with the United States, as witness the European Commission's signal success in forcing alterations in the Boeing–McDonnell Douglas merger in 1997 and, in 2000, blocking the GE-Honeywell merger altogether. In so doing they simultaneously enlarge their margin of maneuver for shaping answers to global problems, such as IMF reform. This is the line of reasoning that enables French policymakers to equate multipolarity with stability rather than competition and conflict. What is frequently characterized—with a touch of yearning—as "the irresistible movement toward a multipolar world" is conceived as a constructive development so long as it is associated with reinforcement of international organizations charged with enunciating and applying common rules of international life. A multipolar world with a prominent place reserved for a unifying Europe would be a safer world if it were also a more fully organized world. In the security domain, that means stressing the "absolute necessity" that an authorizing UN Security Council resolution be obtained before there is recourse to force—by the United States, by NATO, or by anyone else.

French policy has consistently insisted that the authority for taking military action resides with the world body. During the drafting of NATO's Revised Strategic Concept, promulgated at a summit meeting in Washington in April 1999, France parried American proposals that the alliance extend the geographic scope of its strategic interests. The notion of NATO serving as the all-purpose security tool for the Western allies was rejected in Paris on institutional and political grounds as well as legal ones. Jacques Chirac pithily stated the French position: "France will never accept that a regional organization set itself up as a holy alliance to do everything everywhere."[47] Hence the stress on the need for an enabling UNSC mandate is part of a larger strategy for reining in American power.

The emphasis that Paris places on working through the UN Security Council stems as well from the extreme importance that French policy places on developing a constructive working relationship with Russia. Washington's own efforts to prevent Moscow's diplomatic estrangement are recognized. The belief persists, though, that in practice American strategy is too insensitive to Russian amour propre in its eagerness to enlist Russia as a junior partner in U.S.-defined enterprises—including imposing an embargo on the sale to Iran of items that could be used to develop weapons of mass destruction; acquiescing in plans for exploiting the energy reserves for the Caspian basin and Central Asia that bypass Russian territory and control; and signing on to U.S.-led missions in the Balkans. France sees itself as the West's public conscience, ever reminding Washington of the overriding strategic interest the West has in keeping Russia from veering onto the path of autocracy and neo-imperialism. The fact that Germany sees itself as performing exactly the same role does little to diminish France's self-defined duty. The fact that France was the major Western power most ready to sternly criticize the Russians over their excesses in Chechnya further demonstrates this point.

Kosovo

The themes of *multilateralism, legalism,* and *collective responsibility* that run through the French foreign policy discourse are reminiscent of the rhetoric used by the first Clinton administration. The Clinton administration's early hopes of using the UN as a "force multiplier" are matched by France's current penchant for playing the mediator role in building consensual positions as alternatives to American unilateralism. They differ insofar as Washington envisaged multilateralism as a safe method for lightening American burdens, while Paris is attracted to it as a way to extend the range and effectiveness of its influence even while constraining the United States. They are similar in their general desire to strengthen international rule making.

Both countries also have experienced the inevitable tensions between commitment in principle to formal multilateralism and the exigencies of crisis situations. France's starchiness about the UN mandates softened when the alarming developments in Kosovo in February 1999 impelled the quick, decisive action of insisting on a shotgun wedding between Serbs and Kosovo Albanians. The seemingly dogmatic French stance in practice makes allowance for exceptional circumstances. When President Chirac concluded that a replay of the Bosnian tragedy was in the offing unless there were a bold intervention, it became diplomatically convenient to dispense with an explicit authorization by the Security Council. A liberal reading of its early Resolutions 1199 and 1208 judged them "sufficient unto the day."[48] A further referral to the UN carried the risks of delay and possible obstruction by Russia or China and a repeat of the humiliating Dayton experience. There, U.S. diplomats, led by Richard Holbrooke, drove the parties to a compromise settlement for Bosnia while European officials could do little more than observe from the sidelines. A strong Western consensus on the need for harsh measures, sympathetic public opinion, and the absence of overt opposition from any of the major powers facilitated the decision to bypass the UNSC. Still, Minister of Defense Alain Richard made clear France's strongly held view that "all NATO operations not covered by Article 5 should be based on the incontestable authority of the Security Council."[49]

Thus the exigencies of the Kosovo situation can lead to a misreading of French thinking about the importance of enabling UNSC resolutions. France visualizes itself as serving as a *garant* (underwriter) who strives to give international legitimacy to joint actions that the United States spearheads. It is a role that conforms to France's long-standing conception of itself as the dispassionate world mediator. In the years immediately after World War II, French politicians and statesmen were tantalized by the image of a France that kept its distance from both Washington and Moscow, thereby positioning itself to ameliorate tensions by acting as a buffer and go-between. De Gaulle revived the idea of France as an independent force in

European affairs in withdrawing from NATO's integrated command and pressing his own version of détente. France also has visualized itself as a link between the developing world and the wealthy industrial world. The theme of moral obligation to lend a helping hand to the aspiring poor runs through French public discourse about the country's international vocation. It is especially strong on the political left and among some strains of Gaullism, as exemplified by Jacques Chirac.

Mounting dismay at the brutality of the Albanians' expulsions mixed with concern for Western credibility to dictate a qualification of the "prior consent" principle—at least temporarily. Overall, the Kosovo initiative encapsulated the diverse strands of French attitudes toward advancing its own national aspirations, contending with a domineering United States, and exploiting the utility of international organizations. The U.S. hard line on recrudescent strife in Kosovo throughout 1998 raised the unhappy prospect of Washington once again policing Europe and encouraged French leaders to follow an interventionist course. President Chirac's own conviction that Western Europe must not allow a repetition of Bosnia already pointed in an activist direction. In the wake of UN ambassador Richard Holbrooke's apparent success in securing Slobodan Milosevic's acceptance of the ill-fated October accord, Paris had leapt at the opportunity to join Britain in constituting a reserve force in Macedonia that would come to the rescue of monitors from the Organization for Economic Cooperation and Development (OECD), if need be. Convergent problem assessments, agreement on an approach that backed an aggressive search for a settlement with the threat of military action, and the designation of Foreign Minister Hubert Védrine and his British counterpart, Robin Cook, in the name of the EU, as cochairs of the high-pressure Rambouillet conference—all combined to allay latent French apprehension about aligning itself with tough talk from Washington and brandishing the mailed fist of NATO.

The failure of NATO's attempt at coercive diplomacy put French-American cooperation to the sternest possible test. Slobodan Milosevic's resistance to intimidation forced the Western allies to make good on the threat to subject the Serbs to air strikes. Belgrade's retort of brutally driving out the Kosovars caught Western leaders by surprise. The boost given Milosevic's popularity was equally unexpected. The seeming dead end in which Western policy found itself during the two and a half months of frustration and self-doubt could well have spawned division and recrimination. Searching desperately every avenue for a diplomatic way out while debating the merits of expanding air strikes, even if civilian casualties were to increase, allied governments neither broke ranks by venturing into solo diplomacy nor sought to impose panaceas. The contrast with their fractious conduct during the Bosnian conflict could not have been starker.

There were French-American differences. President Chirac actively resisted extension of the air campaign to target sites in Belgrade, especially during the diplomatic endgame, and argued forcefully against strikes in Montenegro. He also made known his displeasure at Washington's failure to advise the allies of stealth bomber and some cruise missile attacks authorized outside NATO's formal integrated command. Those frictions were contained, though, and never threatened to break solidarity between Washington and Paris.[50]

Cooperation between Washington and Paris was thorough and routine. The personal rapport between Presidents Clinton and Chirac, cultivated over nearly four years, set a tone of candor and trust. Communication at the working level—ministry to ministry, staff to staff—was free from the tension that so frequently in the past had distracted and interrupted. Assiduous French efforts to put the relationship on a businesslike footing paid dividends.

The handling of the Kosovo dossier demonstrated two cardinal truths about French-American dealings in general. Foremost is that agreement on objectives is most likely to produce agreement on methods when the rivalry over division of labor and organizational jurisdiction are subordinated to requirements for effective action. The other is that success in making transatlantic multilateralism work in practice eclipses differences of principle (as on the "mandate" question) and brings down to earth rarified conceptions such as multipolarity.

Back to Normal

Kosovo marked the boundaries of pragmatic cooperation between Paris and Washington. Cooperation in the Balkans did not alter the structure of the relationship or usher in an era of enduring good feelings. Differences of approach toward Iraq, the dispute over the United States' national missile defense initiative, and mutual suspicions about the ends and purposes of the EU's fledgling European Security and Defense Policy kept a current of tension running between the two capitals. But the overall tone remained civil, and discordant views were expressed judiciously. The principles of proportional criticism and strategic perspective were observed. Both were more seriously tested with the change in American administration until September 11, 2001.

President George W. Bush's early foreign policy moves widened the gap in thinking about a number of sensitive issues while reawakening French fears of a reversion to American unilateralism. The questioning of the transatlantic understanding on ESDP reached at the NATO and EU summits in December 2000, which supposedly laid to rest U.S. anxieties about a threat to NATO primacy, gave the impression that the incoming team in Washington wanted to turn back the clock on Euro-American security cooperation. Its discarding of the Clinton policy of engagement with North Korea coupled with an adamant commitment to build an ambitious missile defense system, whatever other governments might think about it, smacked of the old-style American arrogance French leaders revolted against and that French diplomacy had sought to mitigate. Dismissive rejection by the United States of the Kyoto Protocol on global warming fits the same unhappy pattern. In contrast, promised cooperation with the Europeans on the Middle East and the abandonment of what the French perceived as a failed policy on sanctions, especially toward Iraq, came as a relief after years of disputes.

The French response to the unilateralist strand of American foreign policy was rhetorically cutting. Paris did take pains, though, to coordinate its criticism with its EU partners and other governments. That approach served well French objectives of building coalitions to countervail unwelcome assertions of American power while keeping open its own lines of communication with Washington. In this sense, the Bush administration's aggressive unilateralism was grist for the French mill as Paris pursued indefatigably its project of strengthening the EU's capacity and will to be an independent force in world affairs. Washington's renewed desire to shed peacekeeping burdens in the Balkans, punctuated by its ceding to the Europeans the main responsibility for coping with the Macedonian crisis in March 2001, served the same French interest. From France's strategic vantage point, Washington's willfulness could be turned to its advantage. For the United States, the question—only partly apprehended—was how to maintain the privileges of unilateralism and selective leadership in a transatlantic atmosphere made less congenial by Europe's post–cold war evolution, in which France was the key player. These privileges might still be retained in regions distant from Europe, as in Afghanistan, but in Europe this would not be tenable.[51]

CHAPTER THREE

NATO:
Lost Opportunities

ALLIANCES ARE MATTERS of self-interest. They must reconcile each party's conceptions of national interest that are convergent but not identical. Although NATO has figured prominently in the foreign policies of France and the United States for over half a century, the two countries have frequently held conflicting views on the alliance's role, functions, and processes.[1]

From the outset, France was never entirely comfortable with the position of strategic dependency on the United States. The lesson drawn by Frenchmen from twentieth-century history is that alliances are useful and expedient tools but should not be counted on wholly for national security. The trauma caused by dependence on unreliable allies has left its mark on the national psyche. This explains in part the attitude that some Americans perceive as prickly defensiveness. The French believe that they paid a heavy price for allowing France to become hostage to its alliances in the first half of the twentieth century. It had relied on a defensive alliance with Britain and Russia (the Triple Entente) before World War I but found the British effort incommensurate with the requirements for containing Germany's assault. France then witnessed with horror the collapse of its ally Russia in 1917. In the 1930s, the British move toward an appeasement strategy, especially in refusing to confront Hitler over the remilitarization of the Rhineland in 1936, is widely recognized as the turning point that put Germany in a position to threaten all of Europe a few years later. In both instances, the inability of France to pursue a more self-reliant strategy led to bloodletting and, in World War II, to occupation and defeat.

The lasting effect has been to make the French extremely cautious about their alliances. That instinct was reinforced for French policymakers by the 1956 ill-fated Suez operation. The lesson drawn was that it was imprudent to rely upon other states where vital national interests were at risk. This conclusion was diametrically opposed to that of their British counterparts. Thus, the French share with Americans a discomfort with "entangling alliances," even though the connotations are quite different.

During the cold war, for France and its European partners, NATO was first and foremost an insurance policy. It provided protection from possible Soviet blackmail by committing American military power, and especially its nuclear capacities, to deter possible Soviet aggression. The value that France placed on the American defense umbrella varied over time, fluctuating with the likelihood of the Soviet threat. Indispensable to the country's security in the 1950s, NATO in the 1960s lost some credibility and utility with détente because the cast-iron character of the guarantee eroded with the Soviet Union's ability to strike U.S. territory. With the deployment of medium-range nuclear forces by the Soviet Union in the late 1970s and early 1980s, France was drawn closer to the alliance—now needed to offset this new threat to European security. The French therefore felt more solidarity with their European and Western partners in a way not dissimilar to the Germans' existing perception of their security. French relations with NATO therefore went through cyclical reassessments, even as the substratum of agreement on strategic needs remained constant.[2]

The end of the cold war accentuated inherent strains over NATO by diminishing in French eyes the overall value of the American security guarantee. For France, as opposed to most of its European partners, the price exacted by the United States for its military presence in Europe was exorbitant. Many of the features of the NATO system had been viewed as excessively "expensive" even during the cold war period. Given that European security no longer was in serious jeopardy, the French saw it as abnormal that the NATO system should continue to be dominated by the United States to the degree that it had been during the period of East-West confrontation. The insurance policy had simply become too expensive.

The integrated command structure was at the heart of French discontent. France found it unacceptable that senior American officers in positions of command were responsible not only to the North Atlantic Council

(NAC)—more generally known as the NATO Council—but also directly to the Pentagon and the president through "double-hatting" arrangements.[3] The Supreme Allied Commander in Europe (SACEUR) is also U.S. Commander in Europe (U.S.COMEUR) and in this capacity has responsibility over an area much larger than that covered by the Supreme Headquarters Allied Powers Europe (SHAPE), comprising as it does Northern and Eastern Africa down to the Horn of Africa as well as much of the Middle East. Furthermore, the ambiguity of NATO Article 5 commitments, mandated by the U.S. Senate, left many Frenchmen uncertain about the solidity of the U.S. engagement. This uncertainty was coupled with the inescapable fact that the United States could at any moment cease providing European security, if not by denouncing the treaty, at least by putting a minimalist interpretation on its obligation, whereas it was clear that the Europeans had no such luxury. It was to protect themselves against such an American opt-out that the Europeans and the United States had chosen, outside the framework of the treaty, to entrust the command of the allied forces in Europe to the American SACEUR. His powers, not unlike those of a wartime commander, remain exceptional for a military leader in peacetime. The term SACEUR, in fact, dates from World War I. The ensuing independence of the American commander from the political authorities of the alliance is greatly strengthened by his responsibility as U.S. Commander in Europe, which gives him authority over an area much greater than that available to him as SACEUR.

Political consultation does exist inside the NATO Council and its subordinate committees, but the dependence of the European nations on the United States (created in part by the geographic imbalance between the two) guarantees in French eyes that these negotiations are very often no more than a formality. As a military organization, NATO confines itself in the main to drawing up plans and organizing exercises. The work of the commands and of a substantial proportion of the civilian organization is primarily to put forward hypotheses and to construct response scenarios, organizing the respective contributions of the various allies in each case. NATO in its military sense—mainly SHAPE—is essentially designed not to implement the military plans that it has formulated, but to enable the United States in the form of the U.S. Command in Europe (EUCOM) to take charge of military operations, using its own concepts and plans as it thinks fit. A posteriori politico-military validation is then supplied by the Military Committee, endorsed if need be by the North Atlantic Council (NAC).

This arrangement allows, indeed in some respects requires, SACEUR to receive his instructions directly from Washington rather than from the multilateral headquarters in Brussels.[4] Moreover, the exceptional prerogatives enjoyed by SACEUR give him control over appointments, budgets, and, especially, equipment. At NATO, the so-called military requirement for Europe is assessed by SACEUR and his SHAPE staff, with the Military Committee and the NAC to a large extent serving to rubber-stamp decisions already made. This system gives the United States a degree of control over NATO military matters that could only be justified in the French view by a serious and manifest threat. This was precisely the reason for France's withdrawal from the military organization in 1966, at a time when the threat was thought by French leaders to have receded.

Still, French leaders were ready to pay a relatively heavy price in terms of autonomy should the situation change for the worse.[5] This state of affairs was tolerated, albeit unwillingly, as an unpleasant but incontrovertible fact of life so long as Western Europe was menaced by the Red Army. The French government did not debate the need for a Supreme Allied Commander in Europe in times of conflict.[6] Its problem was with the maintenance of the exceptional wartime prerogatives of the American military chief in peacetime. Was the confrontation with the USSR a mortal contest? Or was it in effect a period of armed peace, where direct conflict was highly unlikely? If the latter, it was illegitimate and inappropriate to allow SACEUR the large measure of independence from multilateral political oversight that he customarily enjoyed.

The question of how much autonomy the military should have in relation to that of their political masters is a sensitive issue in France. The country's military performance in the twentieth century has been a checkered one. Skepticism about the professional military's willingness to defer to political authority and judgment was compounded by the painful experience of decolonization, during the Algerian conflict in particular. As a result, the French political leadership under the Fifth Republic, backed by the diplomatic establishment, has consistently imposed strict control over military activities, sometimes bordering on micromanagement. The Americans, once unburdened of the Vietnam syndrome, have taken a different stance, allowing their military a considerable measure of discretion, including over matters that the French would view as political and therefore outside the scope of the military. The so-called Powell doctrine, for instance, which implicitly sets the bounds for the engagement of U.S. combat forces, would be totally unthinkable in France inasmuch as it was set explicitly by the United States' chief military officer (when Colin Powell was chairman of the Joint Chiefs of Staff) rather than by his political masters. In NATO, these conflicting conceptions of what constituted proper political control became perennial bones of contention between Paris and Washington, reinforcing France's opposition to American domination of NATO's integrated command.

The United States, for its own part, has always been quite satisfied with the existing structure. It held all major commands. Only its most trusted ally, the United Kingdom, also benefited insofar as it was able to maintain national control over its officers in NATO positions through recourse to the double-hatting system. Germany's officers, in contrast, were and still are fully integrated into the NATO system without wearing a German "hat." As long as the cold war lasted, the United States felt no pressure to reform NATO military structures in any way. Criticism from France was dismissed as motivated only by a desire to curb American influence. Even when military doctrine or concepts needed to be revised, as they were in the early 1980s with the "Rogers doctrine" of Follow-On Forces Attack (FOFA),[7] no serious effort was made to take advantage of these changes to bring French doctrine and planning closer to NATO's. Nor did France express any interest in doing so.

With the cold war's end, that situational logic changed, especially as NATO was drawn into real operations. France's key demand, with some European support, was that the NATO commands submit to political control by the allies as a whole. This line of thinking led to the realization that some of the political-military structures that France had boycotted since 1966 could become useful oversight bodies. The Military Committee—composed of the national chiefs of defense and, in permanent session, their representatives—and the periodic meetings of defense ministers are indispensable for member governments as a conduit for passing on the political instructions of the NATO Council to the military command and the operational judgments of the command to the political masters. In other words it translates political instructions into military language and military considerations into politically understandable language. Activation of these councils was a necessary condition for the collective monitoring of the military commands that France had always advocated. The issue acquired point and prominence after the landmark Oslo ministerial in June 1992, when NATO declared its readiness to become involved in crisis management operations in the Balkans, where French military personnel were already engaged. NATO was gradually evolving into a versatile, more task-oriented organization with a wide-ranging agenda. Intergovernmental deliberations no longer proceeded in the shadow of a menacing Soviet Union. There was more room for divergent problem definitions and threat assessments along with diverse views on how best to deal with them.

The alliance was becoming both more and less egalitarian. Because it was now involved in smaller conflicts, where the important factor was no longer deterrence of a strong adversary but rather the ability to send, support, and sustain smaller contingents in distant operations, the relative status of the United States and its major partners was closer to being on a par than before. However, a distinction was coming to the fore between countries such as France and the United Kingdom, both of which were able and willing to send significant forces into conflicts outside their territories, and other NATO allies, whose contributions could not be as large, either because their capabilities were insufficient or, like Germany, for political reasons.

A more egalitarian alliance between the United States and the larger European nations inevitably meant that Washington would find it harder to get its way on more occasions. France predictably has been in the forefront of efforts to free the alliance's collective policymaking processes from American domination. The United States' perceived bent for unilateralism has motivated France to insist on full and frank consultation within the alliance, strict observance of the decisions made by unanimous consent, the curtailing of the discretionary powers accorded NATO commanders, and the requirement of a UN mandate for taking military action. Agreement at Oslo on NATO's new missions only increased these deep French-American differences. For the United States, NATO could not be restricted to providing technical assets at the service of the Europeans. NATO's involvement carried a price. It was to be the "essential forum for consultation" among the allies.[8] Although France took pains to have the wording qualified by the addition of the phrase "under the Washington Treaty," the interpretation of the clause depended on the meaning placed on the words. For France, the treaty covered essentially mutual defense and meant that NATO should not trespass on the jurisdictional boundaries of other organizations. Naturally, the U.S. conception of NATO's role was more expansive. The restrictive French view eventually lost out in the face of a strong determination by member countries to make full use of alliance capabilities and to ensure an active American presence in European affairs.

A Clash of Two Conservatisms, 1990–95

During the last years of the Mitterrand presidency, the issue of France's relations with NATO was not addressed officially. This conservative approach

differed sharply from growing feelings within the Paris foreign policy community that the status quo did not serve the French interest. President
Mitterrand was reluctant to be seen as jeopardizing the Gaullist heritage,
including even the withdrawal from NATO's integrated command, which he
had opposed in 1966. Mitterrand was far from being an all-out opponent of
the United States.[9] His personal relationship with President Bush was initially good, and the latter took great pains, as spelled out in his memoirs, to
establish a rapport between the two countries.[10] The mood of comity, which
had presided at the bilateral meeting in Kennebunkport, Maine, in May
1991, did not last, however.[11] It was followed by mutual disappointment: on
the part of the Americans because they had understood that France would
make a move toward NATO, and on the part of the French because they had
understood that the Americans were going to make wide-ranging proposals
for changes within NATO. Furthermore, the ostentatious way in which the
United States was celebrating "partnership in leadership" with the Germans
rather than with Europe ruffled feathers in Paris. Washington and Paris
both took a selective approach to NATO issues.

In the end, France's proposals in the early 1990s for revamping European security structures evoked so much suspicion with its European allies
that France had to go along with most Atlanticist initiatives. It did so with
such bad grace that the psychological and therefore political effect was that
its tactical retreats often gave the appearance of political defeat. Furthermore, the underlying suspicion that France's only aim was to organize
European security without the United States undermined the credibility of
its own initiatives for the establishment of European-only security bodies.
The failure of President Mitterrand's pet project for a "European confederation," a vague but spectacularly launched endeavor that was meant to
include Russia but not the United States, fell victim to this suspicion and to
the fear of its domination by Russia in Central European capitals.[12]

Hubert Védrine, in his memoirs of his fourteen years at the Elysée, does
not hide Mitterrand's (or his own) resentment at the heavy political price
that the United States was trying to extract from Europe for its continued
military presence.[13] George Bush himself had put U.S. demands rather
bluntly: "We are not seeking a thirteenth seat at the EC table . . . but we do
see an expanded role for NATO. It will be guaranteeing against instability."
Mitterrand's well-documented reluctance to give in to pressure explains in
part why France was not ready for grand gestures of reconciliation. This
was not helped by a widespread feeling in French diplomatic circles at the
time that any visible and unilateral movement on the issue of NATO would

involve a loss of face, undermining the credibility of French diplomacy on security issues in Europe. In addition, some sectors in the French military were concerned that their special status within NATO, establishing as it did a direct relationship between the French chief of defense and SACEUR, would be replaced and *banalisé* by any change in the French relationship to NATO. From a status of "equality" with the Supreme Allied Commander, as spelled out in the Ailleret-Lemnitzer agreement of August 22, 1967, the French defense chief's status would, it was feared, be reduced to one of "subordination" akin to that of the other allies.[14]

In Washington, in contrast, NATO was perceived as the only institution capable of maintaining the United States as a permanent actor in Europe.[15] The demise of the Warsaw Pact, and soon of the Soviet Union, was not greeted without some anxiety. The institutional arrangements in Europe had been set up in order to contain the Soviet threat. Its evaporation could have led to the conclusion that the cold war institutions had to be replaced.[16] But the choice made by the United States, which was supported by almost all its European allies, was a very conservative one. Fearing that the vagaries of transatlantic relations and U.S. domestic politics could make it impossible to replace the existing system with a modified and permanent pact, U.S. policymakers decided that NATO should remain the cornerstone of their European position. Rather than waiting for the Europeans to give the European Community a capacity in the political and military realms, they preferred to rely on a known quantity.

On the strategic question of retaining NATO as the main forum for consultation on European security issues, the French authorities' initial skepticism was overwhelmed by the support for the organization by its partners. Germany, for one, enthusiastically welcomed the continuation of the NATO integrated system, on which it depended totally for its planning facilities and which it felt reassured its neighbors that German power could never again be used against them. Germany especially applauded the decision, made at the London summit of NATO in June 1990, to open diplomatic contacts with NATO's old Warsaw Pact adversaries.[17] This, added to the "partnership in leadership" stance taken by the Bush administration, led to joint U.S.-German initiatives to strengthen NATO's "outreach" policy, such as the creation of the North Atlantic Cooperation Council (NACC) at the NATO ministerial meeting in Brussels in December 1992.[18] France looked askance at these developments. It feared at the time—in the event correctly—that hopes placed in genuinely pan-European institutions such as the Conference (now Organization) on Security and Cooperation in

Europe (CSCE/OSCE), would be disappointed if NATO's strong drawing power were allowed to distract Central and Eastern Europeans from the CSCE.[19] French policymakers also were anxious lest the "culture" of the integrated NATO command structure "pollute" the minds of Central Europeans, engendering demands for enlargement that NATO at the time had no intention of meeting.[20] It is clear that France lost this battle very early on. Its differences with Germany on European security made it impossible for its leaders to pursue a line that was aimed at diminishing the importance of NATO in Europe. France had too much to lose on other fronts from an open confrontation with Germany. European economic and monetary union, on which France had staked so much from 1990, could not hope to move forward in such a context.

This is why France's rhetoric, as expressed in policy speeches and in diplomatic communiqués, was not matched by its actions. When the day came, the French government generally acceded to the desires of its partners at the eleventh hour. It could not stop NATO's eastward policy or the expansion of its functions beyond a strict reading of Article 5. The latter issue was decided by events in Bosnia. Between 1991 and 1994 it became progressively clear that the Europeans, who had claimed the role of peacekeepers for themselves and had been encouraged in this direction by the Americans, could not enforce a peace without at least some support from the military instruments held by NATO. Thus the French, after voicing some initial reservations, accepted the principle of NATO's involvement in OSCE- and UN-mandated peacekeeping operations at the Oslo ministerial in June 1992. The assets of the headquarters of the UN Protection Force in the former Yugoslavia (UNPROFOR), for instance, were borrowed from NATO's NORTHAG command in northern Germany.

France's dilemma now was practical as well as theoretical. It was contributing the largest contingent to UNPROFOR, the commander of which was a French general. Still, given France's absence from NATO's military decisionmaking system, especially the Military Committee, it had no ability to influence military decisions made at NATO headquarters that could affect the fate of its soldiers on the ground in Bosnia. This pragmatic realization led a growing number of French officials to call for a realignment of French policy. In a striking demonstration of this change in attitude, Defense Minister Pierre Joxe, a close ally of President Mitterrand, publicly declared that France was risking isolation in Europe by continuing its traditional posture toward NATO.[21] Joxe's stance earned him a rebuke by Mitterrand. Yet the very fact that a minister would make such a statement was in itself an illustration of the soul-searching that was taking place at the highest policy levels in Paris.

The parliamentary election in March 1993, which President Mitterrand's Socialist Party lost by a landslide, ushered in a period of cohabitation. The political context was further complicated by the joint leadership of Jacques Chirac, the leader of the governing party, and Prime Minister Edouard Balladur after the 1993 elections and their competition in the 1995 presidential election. Prudence was the watchword as care was taken to keep any contentious security issues out of the political fray and because the Elysée Palace was blocking any move by France that would change the institutional structure of the French relationship with NATO. In one sense, the new political circumstances made it easier for France to shed its erstwhile hostility to NATO's new missions, as well as to NATO's orientation toward Central and Eastern Europe, because the political responses were shared. Cohabitation forced the political left and right to agree on the essentials of the country's foreign relations, the tie to NATO prominent among them. France then participated as a de facto member of the Military Committee in permanent session, if only on issues pertaining to peacekeeping and peace-making activities in which its forces were engaged.[22] This expedient arrangement did not alter France's continued formal abstention from taking an official place on the committee. Indeed, the French attitude at the time was dictated by Mitterrand's desire to preserve the institutional relationship reached in 1966. As long as matters remained discreet and informal, some leeway for change was allowed. Thus many practical matters were handled pragmatically. For instance, in February 1994 French foreign minister Alain Juppé was the first senior European official to call for U.S. political as well as military participation in the international operation in Bosnia, and it was Jacques Chirac during his first presidential visit to Washington in June 1995, following his election to the presidency the previous month, whose "blunt warnings contributed to the re-evaluation of American policy" (of nonmilitary intervention in the conflict), as Richard Holbrooke spelled out in his book on the Dayton peace accord.[23] Still, it remained impossible for the French government to formalize new arrangements. In 1994, toward the end of his second presidential term, Mitterrand was too ill to be informed of Defense Minister François Léotard's participation in an informal NATO defense ministers' meeting in Travemünde, Germany, in 1994 and was reportedly furious both because he had not been told and because Léotard took part. The French chief of defense, Admiral Lanxade, was prevented at the eleventh hour from participating in an informal session of the Military

Committee.[24] His ambiguous status was left undisturbed until Jacques Chirac entered the Elysée in May 1995. Both the mutual suspicion and institutional defensiveness between 1990 and 1993 and the hesitation between 1993 and 1995 left scars that would reopen at the end of the more forthcoming period that followed.

The Chirac Years: An Earnest Attempt to Adapt NATO

Chirac was prepared to proceed with the necessary *aggiornamento* in earnest. But rather than undertake comprehensive negotiations with the allies, which France would in any case have started from a position of weakness, since it had already accepted a NATO role in crisis management, his government chose at first to proceed with small, incremental steps. The full reintegration of France into the command structure would await fundamental changes in NATO structures, above all the establishment of a European identity within the alliance. The new government understood, as most French experts in the field had for a long time, that it was impossible to pursue the goal of creating a European security and defense identity without taking into account the fact that most Europeans would not support such a move if it weakened NATO. Indeed, the condition for their support was that it would maintain the transatlantic link.

In order to achieve such a restructuring, the Chirac government decided to make three unilateral moves. They were intended to show allies, Americans and Europeans alike, that France was determined to be a bona fide transatlantic partner. The prospective reintegration into NATO military structures, though, was in fact conditioned on their adaptation and Europeanization. The moves selected by the French president and announced to the NATO Council on December 5, 1995, were meant to allow France to be in a position to influence NATO decisions without reintegrating the military structure. This is why France formally returned to the Military Committee and decided to allow its defense minister to participate in biannual NATO ministerial meetings and to strengthen its military missions to the NATO commands. In order to accommodate France, the allies resurrected a provision of the Washington Treaty that made it possible to call for the NATO Council to meet at the defense ministers' level, thus avoiding the complication of France taking part in Defense Planning Committee meetings, the substance of which largely had to do with the management of the integrated command. This had the advantage, from France's point of view, of establishing a clear division of labor between the foreign and defense ministers, preventing the creeping tendency of the Defense Planning Committee to become a facsimile NATO Council, without French participation—something that had been such an irritant in former years. The first such meeting, on December 5, 1995, which gathered both defense and foreign ministers in the same room, was judged unwieldy. Defense and foreign ministers henceforth met separately.

The French move was given additional credibility by Paris's constructive role in drawing the United States into a search for a resolution of the Bosnian conflict via NATO. French policy under the leadership of Foreign Minister Alain Juppé from 1994 onward had strongly favored the participation of U.S. ground troops in efforts to end the Bosnian conflict.[25] It gained impetus with Jacques Chirac's arrival at the Elysée and Juppé's accession to the office of prime minister. Their promotion of more decisive military actions to stop the escalating Serb campaign of ethnic cleansing shifted the alliance balance in favor of those advocating direct Western intervention. The takeover of the Verbanja bridge from Bosnian Serbs by French troops in August 1995 under direct presidential orders is a case in point. In this sense, Chirac catalyzed the American initiatives, including the bombing campaign, that led to the Dayton meeting. The experience of the preceding three years had nonetheless induced French and other European governments to prepare for contingencies in which the United States would not take part. It was therefore necessary to envisage options that would allow NATO to provide the structure and resources to allow Europeans to act on security problems by themselves without unnecessary duplication of military resources. This approach tallied very well with traditional French Europeanist views, yet it clearly was meant to strengthen the transatlantic link by enabling the alliance to take action in any likely circumstance.[26]

On one hand, the positions of the key allies' governments were not very far apart. Every country agreed that NATO should adapt to the requirements of the new European security environment. No country was bent on abolishing the existing military structure or on challenging the United States' leadership role. Differences were recognized, but they seemed to be concerned with matters of degree and emphasis, not with fundamentals. But the resulting optimism that mutually satisfactory terms for France's reentry into the NATO military command could be found was misplaced and seems to have developed from a misunderstanding: although unofficially French decisionmakers made it clear that a full reintegration by France into the NATO military command structure was on the cards, the impression in Washington was that this was a foregone conclusion, even though it was well understood that the political packaging had to be made right. There were in fact considerable limits to how far France could go in altering its long-held position on the terms and conditions for doing so. The French president was genuinely determined to Europeanize NATO as a condition for any further move. Also, many in the NATO military structure and the diplomatic and military establishments in Washington and other capitals were quite content with as little change as possible, especially if change entailed allowing the French to take what they felt was their rightful share of senior commands. Furthermore, there was no constituency in France pushing to reverse the 1966 decision. Most security experts favored a relaxation of France's distant attitude toward NATO's military machine, but there was no consensus among them on how far such a rapprochement should go. The president had stated publicly, during the election campaign and afterward, that he was ready to act decisively. However, the positive rewards would have to be visible enough to convince the French body politic that France was reentering a "new alliance."

As Hervé de Charette, the foreign minister, stated: "France is committed to fully participating in a new NATO, in which the Europeans assume a proper share of the burdens and responsibilities, and which opens up to the new democracies to our East while framing a new relationship with Russia."[27] His colleague Charles Millon, the defense minister, wrote in the *NATO Review:* "Our aim should be to combine the advantages of the traditional structure, essentially linked to the criteria of operational efficiency, with the demands of the new tasks, where the relationships between the operational constraints and the political objectives are closer and more complex . . . in strengthening political control and affirming the European dimension within the Alliance."[28] Revalidating the old structure unconditionally thus would have been politically impossible because it would have been portrayed as forfeiting the Gaullist inheritance, a heavy political cost for the first Gaullist president in twenty-one years. Furthermore, it would have been operationally unwise in French eyes.

Obtaining politically visible changes in the NATO structure was made even more difficult by the fact that the political balance in the United States was shifting in the opposite direction. In some quarters, among longtime NATO hands in the State Department and at senior ranks of the uniformed services, there was resistance to altering NATO's command structures and their wide independence from the NAC. Their opinions weighed heavily in an administration that had come to power on a primarily domestic platform. Furthermore, President Clinton's personal history made it difficult for him to pursue policies that went against the grain of established military thinking. Hence going along with French proposals was politically risky. The unreconstructed NATO supporters in the U.S. bureaucracy portrayed French plans for reforming NATO as thinly concealed devices for curtailing U.S. influence in Europe—even as some in the administration clearly valued the French contributions in the Gulf and in the Balkans, as well as in Cambodia, Somalia, and Haiti. Sentiment in Congress, with a few exceptions, supported the traditional NATO as the only safe option and looked askance at changes that might weaken the U.S. hold over the organization. Any weakening of U.S. influence also threatened to erode congressional and public support for the continued U.S. participation in an enlarging NATO. Such Atlanticist stalwarts as Senator William Roth of Delaware and Chairman of the House International Relations Committee Benjamin Gilman of New York were stressing the need for NATO enlargement at the expense of NATO adaptation.[29] That thinking prevailed in Congress as a whole.

After the successful meeting between the two presidents in Washington in October 1995, President Chirac and his entourage concluded that President Clinton had come to believe France's rapprochement with NATO created an excellent opportunity to move the alliance in the right direction.[30] It was not certain, though, that his predilection would be translated into a firm decision to carry out a major structural reform of NATO.

The historic North Atlantic Council meeting in Berlin in June 1996 confirmed that Washington and Paris were narrowing their differences.[31] France did not achieve all it would have liked, but it made considerable headway. This was largely due to the extraordinary convergence of views among the main European allies, especially Britain, Germany, and France. As a senior official who was closely involved in the negotiations put it: "A compromise was found halfway at the Berlin Council: within the NATO structure, permanent staff and headquarters elements would be double-assigned in advance for both NATO and European missions. European force commanders, wearing both NATO and WEU [Western European Union] hats, would be designated within the NATO military structure."[32] There was no agreement, however, on giving the European deputy to SACEUR the designation and the power to lead European operations in case of U.S. absence, or on his ability to play a more significant role than previous deputy SACEURs in the day-to-day running of the command structure. It would be impossible for a military leader to run a command structure in which he was not functionally involved on a permanent basis, which is essential for the implementation of the first goal. Even so, Berlin represented a major

effort on the part of the Clinton administration, under the personal direction of the president, to satisfy Europe's ambition to play a real leadership
role in military operations. President Clinton had to expend political capital in doing so and in maintaining this position against considerable opposition from the uniformed top brass in Washington, especially SACEUR
general George Joulwan, whose press leaks were notorious at the time.

Mutual Disappointment

Little more than a month after the meeting in Berlin, discussions began on
a more global reform of the NATO military structure—one that would have
given major responsibilities to European generals. This negotiation was
handicapped from the start by overambition. There was a mutual misunderstanding of the limitations under which both countries' leaders were
operating. The French felt that the Americans were ready to consider major
changes within the integrated command structure that entailed redistribut-
ing senior commands between the U.S. military and the Europeans. This
impression was strengthened by initial contacts with cabinet-level officials,
whose openmindedness was wrongly seen as a sign of flexibility on the part
of the U.S. government as a whole, including heads of the uniformed services who had assented only grudgingly to the Berlin accords.

The French position was that a significant number of NATO senior
positions should become "Europeanized." This did not only mean that officers from European countries with significant military assets should be
appointed. Rather, it meant establishing a double- and in some cases triple-
hatting system (national, European, NATO) on the model of the United
States at NATO, allowing officers to be in a position to take up NATO commands during European-led operations. Further, it meant that the Europeans should formally nominate them, perhaps through a WEU consensus,
on the model of the U.S. nomination of American NATO commanders.
This also involved giving the deputy SACEUR, whose position would have
rotated among the main European countries, a permanent hands-on post at
NATO to allow him to take over direction of the NATO structure if and
when the Americans decided not to participate in an operation. By the same
token, European generals would be wearing a third hat and rotating in the
same way, in the commands at the so-called regional level: Allied Forces
North and South (AFNORTH and AFSOUTH). Clearly, the change was
more revolutionary in the latter case than in the former, since it involved
taking a prized senior position away from the U.S. military. Still, the post

that would be known as CINCNORTH (commander in chief for northern Europe) would have changed as well, because the German general in charge had until then never been double-hatted. It is noteworthy that the French aim was in fact to modify all these jobs by making them rotational and to triple-hat the officers in charge. France was not singling out the CINCSOUTH position for itself.

If these proposals had been accepted, President Chirac would have obtained the political payoff that he was looking for. NATO's military structure could be said to have been Europeanized and therefore changed to the point where French participation became politically acceptable to all but the most arch Gaullist political elements on the left and right.[33] Since France's position had always been that the Europeans should be more responsible for their defense, its absence from a Europeanized military structure would make such a structure difficult to envisage.[34] The thinking behind the French position was therefore political. It was reported in the French press, however, that the military, and especially Chief of Defense general Jean-Philippe Douin, were eyeing one of the major commands, specifically that of the southern region. The French military's interest in that region was influenced by four main factors: Algerian instability, the desire of President Chirac for France to be more active in the Middle East peace process, the widespread concern among the French foreign policy community about future proliferation of weapons of mass destruction to the south, and the fact that France is the only major military power within NATO whose territory borders the Mediterranean.[35] The French military leadership thought first and foremost of the French national interest. By contrast, the approach of the Elysée, backed by the Quai d'Orsay and the civilian elements of the Defense Ministry, was based on a political desire to further the Europeanization of the NATO military structure. Only after the wide-ranging reform deal discussed in July 1996 fell through did the recommendations of the French senior military converge with the political requirements of the Elysée. At that point, minds seriously concentrated in Paris on the southern command post.

Even then, a certain degree of ambiguity remained, inasmuch as the military leadership was still thinking of the post as France's due, whereas the Elysée-backed political proposal was clearly aimed at rotating this post, along with the northern command and deputy SACEUR, among at least the main three European countries. Hence the severe communication difficulties experienced by the French, whose European strategy was often portrayed— not only in the United States—as a ploy to obtain a major NATO military command for themselves. The difficulties were compounded by the lack of a sufficient awareness on the French side of the restrictions that the upcoming presidential election placed on the U.S. administration. With a Republican-held Congress, and the traditional tendency of the U.S. public to trust Republicans rather than Democrats on issues of national security, it was very hard for the administration to accede to French requests. This was true even when they were backed by other Europeans and openly opposed by none, including the British. In this setting, it probably would have been wiser to wait until the new administration was formed before raising again the issue of the division of responsibilities in the NATO command.[36] In the meantime, it would thus have been advisable to register and implement as fully as possible the gains from the Berlin NATO Council outcome. This would have meant postponing any decisions concerning French reintegration until the implementation of these gains was complete and until they were made effective by the attribution of European responsibilities to the deputy SACEUR. This element, central as it was to the French and French-British plans, was only alluded to in the Berlin communiqué but was nonetheless acknowledged by President Clinton in a letter to Chirac on September 26, 1996. Personal factors also complicated matters, including the difficult relationship between Secretary of State Warren Christopher and Foreign Minister Charette. For instance, Foreign Minister Charette was accused of disrespect for leaving the NATO Council chamber to brief the press just as Secretary General Javier Solana was starting to read a valedictory message of praise for Secretary Christopher. The personal relationship between the two men had never been good. But this episode showed that these hard feelings were adversely affecting the overall tone of French-American relations. For reasons big and small, the fall of 1996 was a very bad period for French-American relations, and as a result the resolution of the relationship issue between France and NATO was postponed indefinitely.

When President Chirac sent his U.S. counterpart a letter on the command issue on August 28, 1996, this sensitive document inevitably fell into the hands of opponents of French views on NATO. After it was leaked, the U.S. administration was forced to take a public position. This was not to France's advantage, because President Clinton would have found it exceedingly difficult to agree to radical proposals concerning NATO during an election campaign. Furthermore, news articles and op-eds suggested that the French were trying to take over the U.S. Sixth Fleet, though it is not in fact under CINCSOUTH's command. Officials in Paris assumed that U.S. official sources had provided this "information" and that it was not an innocent misunderstanding.

Once in the open, the quarrel spun out of control. Not only did it lock the United States into a negative position, contained in Clinton's September 26 letter to Chirac, but it also reduced French maneuvering space. On the political level, the French had never felt that the southern command post was the only possible way to give sufficient visibility to a Europeanization of the NATO command structure. Indeed, after the initial U.S. rejection, French authorities, from Defense Minister Charles Millon to Presidential Senior Diplomatic Adviser Jean-David Lévitte, made less ambitious proposals to their counterparts in Washington. These included a geographic division of the southern region and a functional division of labor broadly on the lines of the ACE/AFCENT/ARRC (Allied Command Europe/Allied Forces Central Europe/Allied Command Europe Rapid Reaction Corps) arrangements.[37] Clearly, however, the political price of a compromise was getting higher for the French president as the dispute became public. Settling for less-than-ideal solutions could entail a serious domestic political cost. The French continued to try to negotiate throughout the fall of 1996. Chirac sent another letter on October 10, to which he added in his own handwriting, referring to the matter of the southern command: "this is of capital importance."[38] It is therefore obvious that the French were ready to explore different avenues, or to play for time by postponing the implementation of the devolution of the post to a European officer for a few years, as long as their U.S. partner agreed in principle.

These proposals were generally interpreted in Washington as signs of overzealousness rather than flexibility on the part of the French.[39] The ensuing prevailing political climate tied the hands of the second Clinton administration's new foreign policy team. One of Secretary of Defense William Cohen's first statements after his nomination to the post was to indicate that the southern command position was not for negotiation. Secretary of State Madeleine Albright took essentially the same position.

The fraught command issue overshadowed the fact that the two countries' divergent conceptions of what the alliance was for and of how it should be managed had come closer. Most strikingly, they had reached the common conclusion that NATO should have a role in managing national crises in Europe. The United States has aimed consistently at strengthening NATO's position as the "essential forum for consultation among the Allies under the Washington treaty."[40] Its fear was of being dragged against its will into crises in which Washington would not carry the necessary weight because the United States had not been involved from the start. This is a theme that American diplomacy has pressed at all NATO meetings since the end of the cold war and that is present in different forms and in generally guarded language in almost every NATO communiqué since 1990.[41] In addition, there was a meeting of minds on the principle of making NATO assets available to the allies for European-only missions.

Combined Joint Task Forces (CJTF) and the European Security and Defense Identity (ESDI)

The failure of the NATO partners to agree was all the more regrettable, for on many issues of European and global security, including those involving NATO, the policies of France and the United States have actually allowed the two countries to narrow their differences. Successive French administrations have perceived NATO as a potentially useful instrument for European security, even if it was unfortunately too heavily dominated by the U.S. military to perform its functions adequately.[42] This is the common thread in the different attitudes France has seemed to hold with regard to NATO since the end of the cold war, the aim of which is to place NATO assets at the disposal of any grouping of its members on a flexible basis. This meant that NATO decisionmaking on political or military matters, including strategic and operational planning, should give a central role to member governments relative to the integrated command structure (and also allow nonmembers contributing to the operation to have a voice, such as Russia in NATO's operations in Bosnia). In this French conception, NATO is viewed as a coalition-building organization, although it would remain an alliance held together by the demanding defense provisions of Article 5. Two early American initiatives launched by Secretary of Defense Les Aspin at the informal defense ministers' meeting at Travemünde in the summer of 1993 were greeted warmly by French authorities as steps in that direction. Partnership for Peace (PfP) was one. PfP made it possible for non-NATO nations to participate fully in NATO-led operations. It would give them the experience of practical, even day-to-day, military cooperation. Handled properly, this could also have made enlargement a less urgent matter, thus reassuring Russia that the new European security arrangements would not harm or isolate that country. Such an approach fits well with the often stated and deeply felt French view that Russia must be included whenever possible in European security structures.

The second initiative pleased the French even more. The Combined Joint Task Forces (CJTF) concept sketched by U.S. officials seemed to be based upon the same premise as French thinking insofar as there was a direct connection between participation in an operation and influence on all aspects of decisionmaking.[43] The envisaged arrangements would give the NATO military the flexibility needed to conduct limited operations involving only a fraction of the military potential theoretically under the integrated command. At the same time, it would make full use of its standing command, control, and communication as well as information capabilities. There was at this stage no plan, and indeed no intention, to make CJTF into an instrument for the Europeanization of the NATO military structure. Rather, the purpose was to emphasize projection-oriented military capabilities with flexible organizational support. That meant reducing the relative weight of SHAPE and creating a closer relationship between the political bodies and the integrated commands, thereby increasing the importance of the Military Committee. The French quickly saw how this project could give teeth to the long-pursued goal of enhancing European capabilities and responsibilities within the alliance. It would also make it easier for the French to align themselves more closely with or even to reintegrate into the NATO military structure,[44] an aim that Bosnia also made attractive to some British officials, especially within the Ministry of Defence.[45] The British, for reasons stemming directly from their Bosnian experience, saw these moves to instrumentalize NATO as a welcome innovation after their bitter clashes with the United States over the UNPROFOR mission in Bosnia. This new British orientation coincided with the French desire to establish ESDI as the basis for eventually refining and implementing the CJTF concept. It was also a harbinger of the shift in British views on the role of the European Union in security matters, which was eventually spelled out by the government of Prime Minister Tony Blair. Paris envisaged mechanisms for enabling a European military entity within NATO by providing access to its collective military assets in instances where the United States would decide not to be involved in an operation.

Making use of CJTF in order to pursue the objective of a European security identity or policy was bound to complicate transatlantic relations. In this apparent meeting of minds between the Americans and the French lay the seeds of misunderstandings. For one thing, the definition of a "NATO asset" was far from obvious. As is often the case at NATO, it is an expression that is used mechanically but whose definition is unclear. In logic, it should have included only assets held by NATO as an organization, or in other words, collectively by the NATO nations. However, most of such assets lay outside the integrated command. Most NATO assets in fact belong to member nations, though they are earmarked to be placed at the disposal of the alliance in case of conflict.[46] Many of the assets that are indispensable for launching a successful operation belong to the United States. In the cold war configuration, this mattered very little. Success in resisting any direct Soviet threat was entirely dependent on the immediate participation of the United States with all its available assets. These were therefore, by definition, assigned to NATO; otherwise, NATO would collapse. There was thus no useful distinction between U.S. assets and NATO assets, even if use of the latter theoretically demanded sanction by the NATO Council. In the new circumstances, however, the opposite was the case: given that the United States was not necessarily going to participate in every operation, the fact that it was the sole owner of important, indeed key, military assets became a crucial political as well as an essential military issue. Whereas in the event of a massive Soviet attack the United States would have automatically placed all of its European-based assets at the service of the common defense, the same procedures would not apply in the case of more limited, out-of-area operations.[47] There was therefore a risk that the Europeans might embark on military enterprises without the necessary means because the Americans withheld some key assets. This would make such operations not only perilous on military grounds but also dangerous for the alliance politically, because the absence of the United States could then be construed as creating an impediment to the operation itself, thus inevitably opening divisions in NATO's ranks. The United States would face a disagreeable alternative between seeming to engineer such a division, with serious consequences for its standing in Europe, or being forced into participation, with potentially damaging domestic results.

A clarification of the CJTF concept was therefore in order, one that would allow the use of NATO-assigned assets belonging to a nonparticipating NATO nation, with the backing of that nation's authorities and of the NATO Council. It also required practical arrangements between SHAPE and the CJTF headquarters, allowing for a devolution of means to those headquarters in a manner that would not undercut the sound military principle of unity of command. At the same time this would not predetermine the command structure by giving automatic leadership to existing NATO headquarters. Such an arrangement could not be easily obtained because it would face bureaucratic turf obstacles in France, at the Pentagon, and obviously at SHAPE. More important, it would necessitate a profound reform in existing structures that only a deep change in prevailing thinking would permit. Such a transformation could only be accomplished over time, even though events might dictate the creation of interim, more ad hoc mechanisms to make action possible before the CJTF system had come of age. Indeed, this is what took place, first with the implementation and stabilization forces (IFOR and SFOR) in Bosnia, and more tellingly with Operation Allied Force, launched by NATO in March 1999 over Kosovo.

Turning the CJTF into practical reality has proven an arduous enterprise that has engaged alliance officers and member governments since that process was set in motion by the Berlin accords of June 1996. The principles and guidelines agreed on in Berlin allowed for the creation of CJTF headquarters functioning within the NATO military structure "under the political control and the strategic direction of the WEU." This arrangement satisfied the French insofar as it allowed for a devolution of NATO means to the Europeans, organized at the time within the WEU, a body in which the Americans were not present. It also had the effect of ending the French attempt to create two separate military systems at NATO, one in which the traditional system would prevail for Article 5 contingencies and one in which a different military apparatus would handle the "new NATO" functions. That attempt to append a "new NATO" to the old organization was effectively abandoned during the negotiations leading to Berlin.[48] This policy shift reflected the limits of consensus with France's German and British partners. France accepted that NATO as a whole would be updated to meet the new challenges of European security and fulfill what became known in NATO circles as the "new missions." The integrated military command structure would be fully part of the new system, even if this logically implied major internal changes.

The Berlin meeting proved to be the high point of French-American defense cooperation. A protracted and strained dialogue on the reform or renovation of the alliance's structures has marked its aftermath. The French concession in the name of alliance unity, coupled with strong hints that France might return to the integrated NATO system, induced some alliance partners to believe that France had also abandoned its pursuit of a root-and-branch reform of the NATO military structure. President Chirac had stated in his August 1996 letter that "as soon as decisions adopted in Berlin, I repeat, as soon as these decisions have been fully implemented, then France will be ready to take back its full place within this profoundly renovated alliance."[49] The French foreign minister had expressed the same views at the NATO Council on December 5, 1995.[50] In fact, the opposite was true: it was all the more necessary for France to obtain visible changes in the NATO system now that it was no longer in a position to claim success on the creation of a "new NATO" distinct from the "old" one. This rendered a

French success indispensable on diplomatic, and especially domestic, political grounds.

French authorities could have set alternative benchmarks to measure such success: political oversight and control of military activities, the creation of new decisionmaking mechanisms to reflect national participation in operations, the reactivation of long-forgotten provisions such as the meetings of major NATO commanders—SACEUR and SACLANT (Supreme Allied Commander, Atlantic)—under the Military Committee chairman. Indeed, they could have chosen to pursue the full functionalization of the military command structure to reflect Europe's new security challenges.[51]

The fact that Europeanization was chosen instead reflects a triple reality. First, it was believed that this was the theme most likely to receive support from France's European partners. Second, it was obviously easier for public opinion and the French parliament to understand the political significance of visible moves toward the Europeanization of the military command than the more intricate and more obscure possibilities that existed in other directions. This was evidently also one of the causes of the later, and ultimately deleterious, decision to concentrate French efforts on a particular military command: AFSOUTH. Third, Europe has become for many Frenchmen, especially in the decisionmaking elite, a catchall response to France's foreign policy quandaries and somewhat of an automatic refuge.[52]

With the benefit of hindsight, it is now clear that the road chosen then did not help create conditions conducive to the fundamental reform that France was hoping for. On the contrary, the NATO bureaucracy and a number of member countries, above all the United States, reacted negatively. The unity of the main European partners that had prevailed in the lead-up to the Berlin meeting fell apart, and eventually intra-European bickering and recriminations were no less prevalent than transatlantic ones.[53] At the time, however, French authorities felt that this was the most likely route for maintaining European accord within NATO while pursuing changes in the military structure that would enable further progress toward French involvement in NATO's military structure.

This error of judgment was all the more regrettable for two reasons. It made it impossible for France to take her full place in the integrated structures. Even more important, it did not put the emphasis on what was most crucial and most apposite in the French criticisms of the NATO military machine—that is, its poor adaptation to the requirements of its new missions. That shortcoming was starkly revealed by the 1999 Allied Force operation over Kosovo, with the consequence that the United States chose to ignore NATO after the September 11, 2001, attack on the United States, in spite of the decision by the alliance to call on its Article 5 provisions for the first time in its history. Such a deficiency could perhaps have been analyzed coolly beforehand if the debates within the alliance had focused on these structural problems. The French might have constructively raised these issues, which other countries with tangible stakes in the NATO-integrated structures would probably have avoided. Thus the alliance as a whole, not only France, may have missed an opportunity to prepare NATO to undertake the missions that its member governments have set for it.[54]

With progress on the command issue stymied, the French debate over NATO subsided at the headquarters, and in France generally. The decision by Paris to foreclose any further move in NATO's direction was made more certain by President Chirac's dissolution of the National Assembly in April 1997 and the ensuing victory of the Socialist-led coalition of Lionel Jospin. The new prime minister had never shown an interest in NATO matters, and the majority of his party had criticized the decisions made by the Juppé government in 1995. Serious conversations, especially between the Elysée and the administration in Washington, continued for a few months, but the political impetus had been lost. Attention centered on the preparation of the Brussels summit, and afterward on the drafting of the new strategic concept that was eventually adopted at the summit in Washington marking the fiftieth anniversary of NATO in April 1999.[55] Meanwhile, France returned for the most part to its traditional role as an internal critic, its usual tribunician posture. This unsatisfactory outcome explains why the issue of France's relations with NATO has likely become too difficult and too costly politically to be raised again, unless political circumstances change. President Chirac feels that he has spent precious political capital in handling the issue personally and that his openness was paid back with damaging press leaks. The fact that his prime minister since 1997, Lionel Jospin, comes from a party that criticized Chirac's moves in 1995 only reinforces the president's prudence. Likewise, the Americans feel that they were led to believe that France was set on reintegrating NATO at a politically acceptable cost to both partners, and they felt let down, and in some quarters betrayed, after having trusted their French partners. This mutual disappointment on NATO has damaged the French-U.S. relationship as a whole because it seems to confirm each side's suspicions of the other's untrustworthiness. The anti-Americans in Paris can point to the failure of what was clearly the most Atlanticist government in living memory in pursuing rapprochement with the NATO structure. The anti-French in Washington conclude with some satisfaction that the French are incorrigible and that it is impossible to take important initiatives in Europe without obliging them to lower their ambitions significantly.

In the lengthy and important debates on the international mandates needed for NATO operations, France voiced vigorously many of the European reservations and thus brought French-NATO relations back to the spirit, if not the form, that had typified them for some thirty years. The need to restart this dialogue in earnest remained as strong as ever, though— as was made evident by the mixed results of Operation Allied Force.[56]

Kosovo: Toward Europeanization

Kosovo reopened the interlaced issues of NATO's integrated command, the political oversight of military operations, and the value of a European security identity. It was paradoxical that Kosovo rather than Bosnia propelled the idea of a distinct European security and defense identity to the top of the EU agenda. The Western Europeans' performance was far more impressive in Kosovo. EU members agreed from the outset on a tough stance against Milosevic's systematic oppression of the Albanians and supported Operation Allied Force without exception. This operation also was noteworthy for the French and German willingness, albeit with considerable reluctance, to act without an explicit enabling resolution from the UN Security Council. France, the country that has most forcefully asserted that a UN mandate is a prerequisite for military action, found it convenient to lift its strict reading of the UN Charter. Still, it can be expected that the mandate issue will remain a bone of contention between Washington and Paris. The development of ESDP likely will transmute it into a Euro-American issue while dulling its sharp French edge.

If the mandate issue was elided in the Kosovo crisis, the issues of command authority and political oversight were put in sharp relief. Tensions generated by differing views on how to conduct the air campaign, and by its inconclusive effect, were temporarily eased when Milosevic decided to accept the terms dictated by the Western coalition. NATO, which was being portrayed as an ineffective machine in urgent need of reform, was once again seen by many observers as indispensable, the instrument without which European security could not be guaranteed. The chorus of criticism heard everywhere during the conflict was followed by a hymn of unqualified praise. Yet in the French view, the failings revealed during this conflict have not been cured simply because the enemy surrendered. They were, and

remain, the consequence of the distance between a politico-military structure suited to the circumstances of the cold war and the political and operational necessities in a European security environment that has turned
upside down. The decision to use air power alone, and to keep the bombers
out of reach of Serb air defenses so as to reduce the risk of losses, put heavy
pressure on Yugoslav society by destroying a major part of the country's
economic infrastructure. That decision can in large part be explained by
American domestic political considerations. But the "collateral," or un-
intended, damage caused by this choice was felt much more acutely in
European countries than in the United States.

The Europeans' ability to shape the design and determine the modalities of the air campaign was restricted not only by their relatively small contribution to Operation Allied Force, but also by the fact that the strategic
and operational planning phases of the operation had been conducted outside the formal NATO framework and at the headquarters of the U.S. Command in Europe. Those arrangements reinforced the predominance of
American officers and American thinking in the NATO command structure. French leaders in particular were sensitive to the fact that the Joint
Chiefs of Staff in Washington at times overrode SACEUR itself. They felt
that the military operation had been led from Washington rather than at the
NATO headquarters in Evere, Belgium. Multilateral consultation could not
be pursued within the military organization, as in principle it should have
been in such a situation, because SHAPE is the place where, in the event of
conflict, the allies tend to line up voluntarily under an American command
that applies its military resources, concepts, and methods to operations in
Europe. The Americans experienced the opposite problem. The alliance,
though dominated at the military level by the United States, indeed remains
multilateral in its political role. In fact, it was in the NATO Council, and by
way of the members' permanent representatives (that is, through diplomatic
channels), that the military operations were monitored and even to some
extent managed on a day-to-day basis. Therefore the feeling spread in
Washington after the Kosovo operation that NATO was, not unlike the UN
and largely due to France, a multilateral organization that excessively constrained U.S. action.[57]

The frustration of the U.S. military and their supporters in Congress
over the restrictions imposed by the diplomatic dynamics of a nineteen-
nation coalition has left a sour aftertaste, all the more irritating because
Kosovo seems to be the model for coalition operations to come, at least
those that mix military and political elements as did Operation Allied

Force.[58] General Michael Short, for one, has extolled the virtues of a coalition of the willing with the United States at its head, as opposed to another war conducted by committee. Looking at the Kosovo experience, he concluded: "If we're going to provide 70% of the effort, then we should have more than 1 of 19 votes." He said that what the United States should say is, "We will take the Alliance to war and we're going to win the thing for you, but the price to be paid is that we call the tune."[59] His is a minority view. But it indicates a latent stress point between France (and indeed Europe) and the United States that could complicate reaching a consensus on the terms of engagement for future operations. Proof of this came when the United States decided to prefer an ad hoc coalition with a limited number of NATO and non-NATO countries to put an end to Osama bin Laden and the Taliban regime in the fall of 2001. Rather than fighting a war "run by committee," which was the U.S. military's perception of the war in Kosovo, they preferred to eschew the NATO structure, although the alliance offered its full support through the use of Article 5.

The vigorous French move to develop ESDP, spurred by the Kosovo experience, is visualized as serving multiple purposes, all of which derive from a perceived overdependence on a dominant yet unpredictable American ally. This logic points to a need to create a distinctive European presence within NATO as well as to establish an autonomous EU-grounded defense entity. Preparation for the latter is, at the level of political psychology, linked to the former. The French government is the only one to make this point explicitly. Defense Minister Alain Richard has repeatedly argued that a European defense serves two purposes: to be able to act independently of SHAPE by creating an option for a self-reliant EU-only operation without recourse to NATO assets; and to "provide for a firm handle on . . . the levers of influence" on a common NATO operation. As Richard has said, "The Kosovo experience has reminded us that each nation weighs on the whole in proportion to its own military contribution."[60] The conviction that a revamping of arrangements for political oversight of military operations is necessary is not held by the French alone. Some of the smaller allies mildly resent the fact that some serious points of difference are sorted out among the United States and its "interested allies"—that is, they are "precooked" by the Quad (United States, United Kingdom, France, Germany) or Quint (same plus Italy) before they are considered by the NAC. They fear a similar pattern taking hold within ESDP security structures. They complain quite fairly that French protestations when Washington takes its own counsel in the name of the alliance give way to intense satisfaction when NATO decisions involve all the four or five major allies. The French then retort that the effective contributions of individual allies have to be reflected in the decisionmaking process.

An enhanced Europe was the logical answer to the question of how France could achieve a more open and egalitarian alliance while at the same time magnifying its own voice on matters of strategy. Months before the Kosovo crisis became acute, French policy took a fresh tack in seizing the opportunity to relaunch a campaign for a NATO-compatible, though not NATO-exclusive, European Security and Defense Policy. It was initiated by British prime minister Blair, who, in a speech at an Edinburgh meeting of NATO parliamentarians in September 1998, signaled for the first time that Britain was willing to consider a role for the European Union in the security and defense field, bringing his country's position closer to that of France. Franco-British consultations, nurtured during their long isolation from and indeed clashes with the United States in Bosnia (and made all the more urgent by the looming crisis in Kosovo), led to a declaration at the U.K.-France summit in Saint-Malo in 1998 and to cooperation at the Rambouillet peace negotiations over Kosovo, which opened on February 6, 1999, and whose proposals were finally rejected by the Serbian delegation on March 19, 1999. The Gaullist aspiration to create a "Europe-puissance" could now be revived in a manner acceptable to the United States.[61]

The series of initiatives, catalyzed by the Anglo-French "Joint Declaration on European Defense" issued at Saint-Malo in December 1998 and culminating in the Helsinki Declaration a year later, set in motion a process aimed at generating the means and the political will for the EU "to play its role fully on the international stage."[62] The European Security and Defense Initiative, now renamed European Security and Defense Policy (ESDP), commits member governments to an ambitious program for building a rapid reaction force at corps level. The aim of what are known as the European Headline Goals is to have in place by 2003 a 60,000-man force deployable within sixty days and sustainable for at least twelve months. A marked expansion in air- and sea lift is projected to make the force operational. A complementary set of mechanisms for directing military operations and conducting a concerted diplomacy is being put in place. Detailed provisions for reinforcing the ESDP were formally approved at the Intergovernmental Conference at Nice in December 2000.[63] If France has been accused, sometimes rightly, sometimes wrongly, of skepticism toward NATO, the same cannot be said of its major partners. The positions of the French, British, and German governments on the institutional aspects of

European security were now closely aligned for the first time since France
left NATO's integrated military structure in 1966.

The process set in motion at Saint-Malo is in keeping with the spirit as
well as the letter of the 1996 Berlin agreement. According to the Berlin compromise, the Europeans can use NATO assets in operations in which the
United States decides not to participate, as long as this use is sanctioned by
the unanimous consent of the NATO Council. The Europeans in effect have
substituted the EU for the WEU.[64] Meeting the EU's Headline Goals would
create an option for European governments to act on their own, though
that is not their preference. It is clear after Bosnia and Kosovo that the participation of the United States in crisis management operations is not only
desirable but actually sought after—by France as well as other allied governments. An absent United States could make the task of the Europeans
harder by withholding political as well as tangible assets or by offering critical comments from the sidelines (at times for domestic reasons). In French
eyes, the primacy of NATO is therefore essentially a function of the
American need to ensure support at home for U.S. participation in efforts
to resolve crises in Europe.[65]

There is a consensus that when the Europeans decide to undertake a
crisis management operation they will have to go through NATO before
activating purely EU capabilities and structures. The French do not dis-
agree, for they recognize the need for NATO assets to ensure the operation's
success. This logic, embedded in the 1996 accords, is now elaborated in the
NATO-EU framework agreements. In the unlikely circumstance where these
assets were not needed, the French view is that the Europeans would be free
to use their institution of choice. For France, that means the European
Union. France has further envisaged the possibility of European operations
without recourse to NATO or U.S. assets. That scenario could lighten the
burden of the United States for European security if it came to fruition, but
would also reduce American influence.

These issues were thrashed out in intense diplomacy over two years that
culminated in December 2000. Together, at the EU Council summit at Nice
and the NATO Council meetings, the defense ministers and foreign ministers sealed a complex set of agreements that conferred status on ESDP while
linking it closely to NATO structures. The terms of association between
NATO and the newfound EU security bodies represent a Euro-American
bargain.[66] ESDP's functional independence is circumscribed by its enmesh-
ment in a dense network of arrangements for consultation and coordination between the EU and NATO. The EU made that concession in exchange

for firm assurances that it will have guaranteed access to NATO assets for any future EU-led operations, a condition long unfulfilled because of Turkish opposition and now made uncertain by Greek reservations. This reconciliation reins in more unrealistic conceptions of ESDP even as it places the alliance's seal of approval on the European enterprise. The precise specification of how the two organizations will relate to each other notwithstanding, ESDP's evolutionary path and ultimate destination are not entirely within either Washington's or France's control, for Paris has won the approbation of fellow EU governments on the principle of creating an autonomous European security entity by reaffirming NATO as the West's major defense instrument for common and concerted defense policies.

As long as ESDP is developed with the proper amount of coordination with NATO, as desired by the European partners, it should not be viewed as detrimental to a United States that seeks to remain a European power that selectively chooses its military engagements. By placing the emphasis on capabilities, ESDP may serve to rebalance the alliance in a way that supports both American and French interests. The evolution of thinking in the Jospin government, which was initially rather dismissive of French rapprochement with NATO, confirms the strong situational logic that points French policy along the path chartered by ESDP. It is noteworthy that ESDP is within the parameters set by the NATO allies in the Defense Capabilities Initiative agreed to at the Washington summit in April 1999. The requirement by the European allies to improve their force projection, precision and guidance weapons, and intelligence and surveillance capabilities has been stated repeatedly by U.S. officials.[67]

To the French, this emphasis could only lend greater Atlantic legitimacy to the new initiative, which many believe is the only possible way to persuade European treasuries to increase spending on defense procurement.[68] The Kosovo operation made obvious this growing gap between European and American armed forces. For that reason, the French authorities found illogical the skeptical or outrightly hostile reactions to ESDP from some in Congress and elsewhere in Washington's foreign policy community.[69] In October 1999, President Chirac asked rhetorically, in a speech to an Atlanticist group, how Europe could be expected to carry a greater share of the European defense burden when it was ridiculed for possessing an insufficient number of high-performance weapons and yet criticized when it attempted to overcome these shortcomings.[70] It is healthy that the debate has now concentrated on capability rather than organizational jurisdiction and precedence. That focus takes some of Washington's critical pressure off

France because it is Germany, among the big three, that has difficulties maintaining a sufficient defense budget.

The ESDP project does not represent a French victory as much as a necessary rapprochement between the positions of the main European allies. For France, this is part and parcel of the growing Europeanization of its foreign policy. Ironically, this has happened under the leadership of a Gaullist president.

As the NATO-EU framework agreement demonstrates, the French and American conceptions of the Europeans' role in managing European security are reconcilable. France admittedly is a strong advocate and mover for European autonomy, though it could not and would not curtail the United States' prerogative to take part in any conflict management operation. The United States is clearly in favor of NATO retaining its paramount role, though not to the degree that it would automatically carry the greater military burden in times of crisis. On that basis reconciling the two countries' positions should not be beyond the realm of imagination and prudent diplomacy.

CHAPTER FOUR

High Tension:
The Economic Dimension

FRENCH-AMERICAN CLASHES in the security realm are not simple conflicts of interest. They stem from the countries' different locations in the international system, their historical experiences, and their intellectual traditions. Clashes in the economic realm have equally deep and diverse roots. Objective changes in the world economy sharpen the contrasts. Today's global political economy is characterized by the dynamic tension between two distinctive institutions: the state and the market.[1] The shifting locus of action and influence toward the latter poses a paradoxical challenge to all governments. It is particularly acute for the government in France, where traditionally the state has been viewed as an important generator of economic development and widely seen to be a provider of material well-being for its citizens.

France's great prosperity of the past half-century is due in large measure to its participation in a functionally integrated and ruthlessly efficient system of global commercial and financial exchanges. Raw materials, capital, technology, manufactured goods, and skilled manpower move readily across political boundaries. The transcontinental networks woven by open markets and multinational corporations threaten to outstrip the means for their management—certainly purely national ones. That unsettling reality poses two challenges for French leaders. One is to reconcile the discrepancy between the country's collective historical self-identity and its ambition to demonstrate its prowess as a technologically advanced economic powerhouse. The other is to reconcile both identity and ambition with the inescapable realities of European integration. France is widely seen as a stronghold of traditional economic life embodied in agriculture and the crafts despite its outstanding capabilities in many sectors of high technology.[2] That image is central to France's collective personality. But cherished visions of village and atelier coexist with pride in mastering the modern technologies that produced the striking industrial achievements of the postwar decades. The two are imperfectly harmonized. To stand tall in today's high-tech world is to shed much of what has been a reassuring national consciousness.

Europe is both an answer to these challenges and a contributor to a sense of vulnerability. For the country's elites, the Europeanization of economic management is desirable as well as necessary. Their identity is bound up with France's success in holding its own against the Americans and the Japanese, the pacesetters of the international economy of the 1980s and 1990s. Europe makes that possible. A quintessential expression of this outlook was provided by Jacques Delors: "What we need are anchorage points we can hang on to, we need our nations but we also need to build Europe because, contrary to what some say, European construction is not the Trojan horse of globalization but the very element which permits us to adapt ourselves to globalization."[3] The paradox is that to regain a measure of control over the anonymous workings of the world's markets—and to enhance competitiveness—by strengthening multinational bodies would also circumscribe the powers of the French state. Empowering the supranational institutions of the European Union (EU) establishes it as a global force for order and stability. But France has had to relinquish a good portion of its policy autonomy in the bargain and to qualify its attachment to the Colbertian tradition.[4]

Those derogations from the historical norm of state-centered economic management leave unaltered the political verity that Paris is still held accountable for economic outcomes. What citizens expect from the providential state is constant, while the forces of globalization make it harder and harder for the state to deliver. Indeed, the awareness that today's unprecedented prosperity depends on the incomprehensible workings of world markets generates anxiety rather than confidence about its permanency. The resulting demands for reassurance and the protection of entitlements against anonymous economic forces places France's politicians and officials in a quandary. They find it politically difficult to acknowledge their relative impotence before a citizenry unprepared to accept the implications. This is especially so given France's dirigiste traditions. Despite the gradual erosion of the public sector through privatization of state-owned enterprises, the government remains dedicated to guiding key sectors. It does so through the leverage provided by "golden shares" decided by the Socialist government, which entitled the state to exercise proportionally greater voting rights. This is the case, for instance, for Thomson-CSF (now Thalès), France Telecom, and Dassault. Repeated proclamation of that dedication reinforces the public's sense that the state is looking after their interests.

The vulnerabilities—real and imagined—created by competitive forces from all points on the horizon are a universal phenomenon. The dynamism of the global economy heightens insecurities even as it generates wealth and opens opportunity. Wonder at its beneficence is tinged with dread. The balance between the two reactions varies. The optimistic expectation of bounty prevails in the United States; France is more apprehensive. Hubert Védrine depicts a France made fretful by "the rising waters of the global economy, Germans' nightmares, and injunctions from Davos sounding in its ears like the incantations of vespers."[5] The two countries view the globalization phenomenon from antithetical philosophical vantage points. In the American tradition, free markets are natural and they are good. In the French, they are suspect, a blessing when properly managed through "regulation," a disruptive force when unsupervised. Consonantly, the two countries advocate contrasting responses to the question of how best to reconcile the growth imperative and efficiency standard, on the one hand, with the value of stability on the other. An additional source of tension arises from France's position as the most influential and assertive player in a European Union that increasingly vies with the United States to set the ground rules for the great game of world economic competition—today in the commercial sphere, tomorrow in the monetary sphere.

Head to Head?

International economic issues have gained saliency because of the coincidence of market globalization and the centrality of economic issues in domestic politics. Success in satisfying the electorate's expectations of ever-rising disposable income can make or break a government. The primacy of economics is all the greater in France, where a social market philosophy places less responsibility on the individual and more on the collectivity to meet citizens' needs. That responsibility goes beyond prudent macroeconomic management. It includes creating conditions favorable to job creation and direct employment by the state, whether in civil service or the still substantial public sector of state-owned enterprises. Those enterprises, together with the civil service, provide employment for roughly one in four French workers. Moreover, there is near universal agreement that the government should foster wealth-generating economic sectors by financing research and development and capital subventions, establishing preferential purchasing policies, and providing export assistance and some form of oversight. Outstanding examples of industries for which it has done so are electronics, aviation, space, telecommunications, and energy, all of which are critical to national economic security. The names of Airbus and Ariane testify to the success of this approach. The government used to do the same for banking, too. Traces of this were evident in the government's sporadic attempts to play the role of honest broker in the wave of controversial competitive takeover bids that embroiled the country's largest financial institutions in 1999. The state also is the paternal provider of welfare. The wide-ranging benefits made available by Paris serve the dual purpose of guaranteeing access to services regardless of employment status or income while putting in place an extensive, fine-mesh safety net as insurance against the most painful consequences of market-induced dislocations. Much that occurs in the economic life of France falls within the realm of public responsibility—whether the state is promoter, guardian, employer, or insurer.

State influence over the economy is weakening, slowly but inexorably. Sharpening competition and cross-national alliances are exposing France to the forces of globalization. That hard truth was exemplified by the Michelin affair that caused the socialist government of Lionel Jospin such consternation in mid-1999. The world-renowned French tire maker shocked French citizens by announcing plans to lay off 20 percent of its workforce worldwide at the very time that it was registering unprecedented profits on its balance sheet. Roundly criticized by the government in Paris, the Michelin management defended itself by pointing out that cost savings were dictated by a combination of market pressures and demands for increasing shareholder value. An exasperated government could do little more than vent its frustration by chastising the leadership of a firm with a socially insensitive corporate philosophy.

The Michelin affair revealed that 30–40 percent of the shares in blue-chip French companies are in the hands of foreigners (mainly institutional investors, the biggest stakeholder being the California Public Employees Retirement Fund) who do not share the country's traditional feelings about the *gestion paritaire*—the principle of owner-worker solidarity. The government's case was not helped by the nearly simultaneous news that Renault, in which the French state is still the largest shareholder, made known its own plans to slash jobs at recently acquired Nissan Motors in Japan. Renault previously had come in for heavy criticism when it announced in 1997, during the parliamentary election campaign, that it was closing down a profitable plant at Vilvoorde in Belgium.

France's inclination to monitor and, where possible, to manage its external commerce is a natural corollary to the traditions and practices of the dirigiste state. External commercial and financial relations have always been high on the foreign policy agenda. Often that has contributed to disputes with trading partners—particularly the United States. In that country, in contrast, Bill Clinton's successful bid for the White House by relying on the mnemonic slogan "It's the economy, stupid" exemplified, while exaggerating, the newfound primacy of economic welfare issues. Would the United States resort to the predatory practices of a declining hegemon to put parochial American interests first? Would the White House find it expedient to use aggressive tactics in dealing with commercial partners and allies now that the strategic imperative of maintaining Western solidarity to contend with the overriding threat posed by Soviet communism was no longer controlling? The French thought that they knew the answer. The United States would throw its full weight into a campaign to bolster American exports by means fair or foul. Bill Clinton, although an avowed partisan of free markets, publicly declared that he foresaw the battles of the post–cold war world being fought on the terrain of international commercial competition. His twin commanders for the campaign were U.S. Trade Representative Mickey Kantor and Secretary of Commerce Ron Brown. The geographic scope of their strategy looked to be unlimited. They broadcast the tough message that the days of U.S. benevolence were over. Uncle Sam would pull no punches in promoting American interests, their tough methods pursued with single-minded dedication. François Mitterrand, for his part, visualized "a bloodless war with the United States, an economic war."[6]

The wave of trade disputes that crested in the mid-1990s and that has continued to unsettle Franco-American relations is inseparable from trends in the broader economic environment. France has felt itself under a triple threat: a powerful United States less inhibited about the methods it uses to promote its national interests while pressing others to adopt its liberal economic model; a unified Germany that feels less constrained about exerting its economic influence within the EU and newly accessible hinterland to the east; and the gathering forces of globalization exemplified by Japan, the

Asian Tigers, and China, the looming giant. As in the security realm, French policy struggles to pursue a strategy that works while conforming to national norms. Here, too, Europe is both the potential answer and itself a potential problem. Washington's perceived reversion to commercial unilateralism, its conduct at once erratic and provocative, magnifies the significance of building Europe. Only the EU has the weight to check American power. Only the EU could enable France to contain and channel the forces of globalization and restore a measure of keenly sought order to a world economy that literally is out of control.

The Uruguay Round

France's desire to use the EU as a force multiplier to advance its interests, without sacrificing its core interests to a collective policymaking process, took concrete form during the protracted negotiations of the Uruguay Round trade talks concluded in 1993. France's challenge is manifest, too, in the new age of trade diplomacy ushered in by the creation of the World Trade Organization (WTO). The EU's intricate arrangements of shared responsibility for setting a common community position among the intergovernmental Council of Ministers, the EU Commission as a whole, and the individual commissioners in charge of specific portfolios (such as trade and agriculture) opened opportunities for France's skillful diplomacy. Paris benefited as well from having Frenchmen in key EU positions, not least Commission president Jacques Delors and his corps of influential staffers headed by Chef de Cabinet Pascal Lamy (who became the EU trade commissioner in 1999). As the rolling negotiations moved toward conclusion in 1992–93, a handful of obstacles stood in the way of a historic accord whose centerpiece was a World Trade Organization equipped with greater power to enforce an expanded set of rules. Outstanding among them was agriculture. That thorny issue pitted the United States against the EU. At its heart was the community's Common Agricultural Policy (CAP), which provides subsidies to farmers through price support mechanisms that allow them to keep export prices lower than production costs would dictate. French farmers as a group have been its greatest beneficiaries—the recipients of roughly 20 percent of the program's total outlays—while contributing a substantially smaller fraction to the CAP fund.

The United States' demand that the subvention of exports be sharply cut back sparked an acrid dispute over whether, how, and how much the CAP should be reformed. The United States also provides financial aid to its farmers, but mainly through the mechanism of income adjustments that compensate for differentials between market prices and benchmark prices. The dispute epitomized the triangular relationship among Paris, Brussels, and Washington that at once complicates and offers a vehicle for possible resolution of French-American commercial conflicts.[7] The CAP question, a longstanding bone of contention, loomed all the larger for its being the major stumbling block to a comprehensive trade accord. The United States relentlessly attacked it as a gross violation of free-trade principles that cost American farmers billions each year in lost export sales. The Clinton administration insisted on a phased reduction of the CAP support payments so as to cut back mountainous overproduction, a portion of which was "dumped" on world markets. In late 1992 the French government of Socialist prime minister Pierre Bérégovoy, backed by President Mitterrand, firmly resisted American pressures while working assiduously to dissuade its EU partners from offering what Paris saw as excessive concessions. French officials believed they were defending an essential national interest. For French leaders, agriculture stands for much more than just one economic sector among others to be defended against self-interested American demands made in the name of laissez-faire principles. It brings together those elements that arouse French sensitivities about its identity and independence.

Farming, rural culture and all that it connotes for the French national psyche, is a more powerful social and political factor than in other Western societies.[8] Twentieth-century French demographics are one reason for the vividness of evocative rural imagery. At the outbreak of World War II, agriculture provided the livelihood for one of five working French citizens. That figure dropped sharply in the postwar decades of rapid economic growth, largely thanks to CAP. But the rural consciousness lingers on. So, too, does the political influence of farmers. Although they now number fewer than 1 million, they still hold a key political position. Both the left and the right have their traditional bloc of rural voters. The danger that a significant fraction might abandon their party allegiance and switch sides (or stay at home on election day) makes them a major electoral force.[9] Ever ready to resort to extralegal methods to make their point (and enjoying the sympathy of a wide swath of the general populace), farmers form a constituency that every French government must reckon with. To accept drastic reform of the CAP was to provoke a wave of demonstrations across France and damage the political fortunes of those who surrendered a portion of the French soul to foreign interests. In addition, external agriculture sales were a major contributor to a healthy balance-of-trade surplus. Sentimentality and pecuniary interests were bonded to fashion an outlook compelling to the French, but one that looked like obstinacy in defense of self-interest to many outsiders—especially Americans.

The face-off with the United States over CAP reached a critical juncture in November 1992. In what was meant to be a climactic meeting in Washington, U.S. and EU negotiators reached a preliminary agreement (the "Blair House accord") that provided for a modest reduction of CAP subsidies over time. Sir Leon Brittan, the commissioner responsible for the community's external trade relations, led the EU delegation and initialed the agreement in the community's name. In the resulting storm of protest in Paris, Brittan was accused of selling out vital French interests and of doing so without proper authorization. According to France's interpretation of its principal trade negotiator's powers, he needed an explicit prior mandate from the Council of Ministers before making any concessions on the structure of the CAP. At a tumultuous ministerial meeting, Brittan was chastised as a mere bureaucrat who had the temerity to bargain away a French national interest. Most community governments were inclined to think otherwise. Commission president Jacques Delors did not pronounce on the matter, discreetly choosing to act as conciliator.[10] For the French government, the Blair House accord struck like a bombshell, coming just two months after the bitter debate over the Maastricht Treaty on European Union, which had won approval by the narrowest of margins in a nationwide referendum. It threatened to obliterate the Socialists in their already uphill campaign for the legislative elections upcoming in March. Caution was the watchword. The menace to France's faltering support for the entire Maastricht project posed by CAP reform was the most persuasive French argument in the successful campaign to reopen the accord with the United States. It was a dogged diplomatic process that occupied two prime ministers: Bérégovoy and his center-right successor, Edouard Balladur.

Paris's distress about the Blair House accord was aggravated by the complaint that Sir Leon Brittan had allowed his alleged pro-American sympathies to influence his judgment as to what was a good deal for the EU—and for France. Distrust of "Anglo-Saxon" plots to thwart continental enterprises that could challenge their supremacy bubbles just below the surface of French political discourse. On occasions that pit France against a Washington-London coalition (or, as in this instance, when a Britisher in a European capacity is taken to be a coconspirator), those feelings are vented often with an emotion that leaves Americans nonplussed. The stereotyping of Brittan skewed French interpretations of what had occurred at the Blair

House negotiations. In fact, at that time he was far from an admirer of the United States, and his relations with his American counterparts would deteriorate over the life of the negotiations to the point where they were coolly cordial at best. The main characteristic he shares with the Americans is a philosophical leaning toward classical liberal economics.[11]

In the fall of 1993, a year after the short-lived Blair House agreement, the crisis over CAP came to a head in a confrontation between the Clinton administration and a divided EU. The commission's room for compromise was narrowed by the French dedication to holding the line against American pressure. Paris, under the Balladur government, appeared ready to go to the brink. With the year-end deadline for completing the Uruguay Round approaching, the agriculture issue seemed insoluble and the talks on the verge of a breakdown when Delors declared that the gap between the two sides was unbridgeable. Delors reflected French sensitivities about Uncle Sam's penchant for throwing its weight around by reacting strongly to truculent statements by the White House. He described President Clinton as "a man flexing his muscles before a mirror to convince himself of his strength." That was not the opinion of Peter Sutherland, the commissioner for agriculture who was now the EU's interlocutor with the Americans. His plea that a compromise formula was within grasp allowed for an eleventh-hour attempt to renegotiate the Blair House accord (something that Paris opposed).[12] Sutherland's judgment was confirmed; the last impediment—a dispute over the level and duration of community export subsidies for rapeseed oil—was overcome thanks to a retreat by Washington. French stubbornness had won the day, and French diplomacy deserved admiration for bending the EU to its will and thereby setting the stage for a climb down by an American administration unprepared to jeopardize a historic advance in building an open world trading system over a relatively minor matter.

The rapeseed affair reveals asymmetries in the French-American relationship observable in other policy spheres. At the end of the day, Washington was unprepared for a showdown with France (via the EU) both because the interest at stake was less salient for the United States and because it felt obliged to move the entire process forward. In reduced form, the U.S. commitment to creating public goods for the international system persists even as the political environment has forced a rethinking of the particular American interests Washington will sacrifice on behalf of the collective good. The domestic scene, despite the rise of protectionist sentiment, still permitted a relatively enlightened formulation of the national interest in 1993. In this instance, the timing was propitious. The bitter battle over the

North American Free Trade Agreement (NAFTA) drained political passion, allowing the WTO treaty to sail through a distracted Congress. Objective economic factors also helped. The depth and diversity of the American economy dilutes the importance of any product or sector; the greater tolerance of geographically mobile Americans for dislocation in employment together with a political philosophy that minimizes the state's paternalistic obligation to protect them give the executive a wider margin for discretionary judgments while lowering the potential political costs for exercising that discretion. Farm lobbies, rapeseed growers in the lead, did seek to stiffen the American negotiating position. They had the ear of Agriculture Department officials and a direct line into the Office of the U.S. Trade Representative. But they lacked their French counterparts' clout and the evocative symbolism for making their plight a national cause. News coverage was scant, comprehension of the rapeseed oil issue in political circles close to nonexistent. In France, by contrast, the dispute was front-page news. It was featured in other European capitals as well. The French were able to coalesce support within the European Community by drawing on governments' instincts to maintain solidarity—even though several believed the French had pressed their case too far.

The Clinton administration's bark had been worse than its bite. In its confrontation with the EU, it made the major concessions that resolved the stalemate. Those concessions may have been larger than the Balladur government expected, and they were made weeks before the deadline, relieving the pressure on EU governments to seek accommodating terms of compromise or to make offsetting concessions on other contentious issues. Indeed, the American negotiators refrained from any strenuous effort to pursue a linkage strategy. They did so in large part because of Washington's fear that the talks might collapse unless the United States took on the job of clearing away obstacles to an accord. Senior American officials had concluded that the "irresponsible" position of its allies or partners would not give way to Washington's view of where the path of enlightenment lay. Consequently, at no time did the Clinton administration seriously consider holding the EU to the collective commitment it had made with the United States in the Blair House accord.[13]

France's successful defense of its agricultural interests (matched by its obtaining a "culture exception" for audiovisual products) highlighted as well the complexities of France's European "equation." The EU is valued as a critical force multiplier, yet it can become a threat to French interests when it exercises its powers to advance positions that diverge from those of Paris.

France's strategy for minimizing that danger is to insist that the Council of Ministers (the EU's highest intergovernmental body) retain broad authority to set the parameters within which the commission may use its discretionary judgment and to emphasize the council's oversight functions. Implicit is the belief that Paris has an unsurpassed ability to play the intricate game of council politics to its advantage—a constant in French thinking about its place in the community. Even though France has been remarkably successful in acquiring EU support for its interests, it is often anxious about the mounting power of the EU's supranational institutions. That anxiety is omnipresent among political elites and percolates through French society as a whole.

French apprehensions about the EU Commission's negotiating in the name of member governments on matters of international commerce has risen with the establishment of the single market, which came into being in January 1998. Hence France has strained to retain for the intergovernmental Council of Ministers the authority to limit any commissioner's negotiating brief. Similarly, the commission's ambitious proposal in early 1998 to create a New Transatlantic Marketplace (NTM) was derailed by Paris for fear that it would promote trade liberalization at the expense of sensitive French interests. The NTM initiative was the brainchild of Leon Brittan, itself enough to raise suspicion in Paris. Its goals were the creation of a free-trade area in services, the removal of contentious technical barriers to trade through mutual recognition agreements of each side's administration of health and environmental standards, and a further liberalization of existing accords covering investment, public procurement practices, and intellectual property rights. In a bow to French sensitivity, agriculture and audiovisual services were excluded. The American reaction had been guarded. With protectionist sentiment on the upswing in the Congress, a wounded President Clinton remained reluctant to promote a contentious set of trade liberalization measures. Any well-meaning attempt to clear the air by giving renewed political momentum to Euro-American economic cooperation would never leave the launchpad.

The French scuppered the plan by putting a political roadblock in its path at a Council of Ministers' meeting on March 30. President Chirac and Prime Minister Jospin joined in arguing that the scheme was an ill-considered attempt to circumvent the council's authority and barred its presentation to the United States at the biennial EU-U.S. summit in May.[14] They justified their opposition by arguing that a far-reaching transatlantic accord could jeopardize multilateral talks under WTO auspices. France was not alone in its unhappiness about the liberty the commission was taking vis-à-vis the Council of Ministers but, as is frequently the case, it was the most vocal in condemning it publicly. A disappointed Sir Leon protested what he called "intemperate and unreasonable" French criticism. In keeping with the dialectic of Brussels politics, he relaunched a more modest "action plan," renamed the Transatlantic Economic Partnership (TEP), within a few months. It aimed at establishing collaborative mechanisms whereby the United States and the European Union would work to anticipate and resolve disputes arising from incompatible regulatory standards and procedures. France, having won the battle against a comprehensive trade negotiation that could endanger French interests and having reined in a freewheeling EU Commission, was ready to give its contingent approval to a more controlled, step-by-step technical exercise.

The practical approach has ameliorated Franco-American tension and improved the tenor of the transatlantic dialogue in general. In 1999 the EU and the United States set in place an "early warning system" to identify and consult on regulatory or legislative actions that could generate trade frictions. They also prepared the ground for mutual recognition of each other's licensing, certification, and accreditation procedures to expedite the liberalization of trade in services ranging from insurance to engineering. The bruising battles of the preceding years over relatively minor matters had exacted a heavy toll on transatlantic amity. Washington and Paris recognized the need to concentrate on constructive problem-solving in a less contentious mood. Both the Clinton administration and the French government gave their good-faith backing to the initiative. Neither conceded intellectual ground in their ongoing debate over what conception of open markets should govern trade rules, and no formula was found to deal with the sensitive issues of audiovisual commerce and agriculture. The 1999 talks in Seattle on setting an agenda for the Millennium Round of trade negotiations had a similarly unhappy outcome.

The course of least resistance can also be sound policy. The suspension of debate on a thorny issue avoids the risks of negative spillover. That logic holds if the problem does not fester and make reaching an accommodation all the more painful when the issue is revisited. That risk depends in part on intervening variables: domestic political developments on the American side; EU and domestic developments on the French side. On agriculture, actions taken at the European level carry the potential for reducing tensions. The EU's "Agenda 2000" reforms, intended to prepare the ground for enlargement to the East, addressed proposals for scaling back the CAP, a move the United States would welcome. At the March 1999 EU summit in Berlin, however, only modest adjustments were made. Staunch French resistance to proposals for large cuts in guaranteed prices prevented the promulgation of plans for a far-reaching reduction of CAP outlay. The French "redesign" of the reform package ensured that agriculture would continue to be a sticking point in Franco-American and U.S.-EU trade relations.

The Boeing Affair

Initiatives originating with the EU Commission can also activate latent issues. A striking case in point was the decision by Karel van Miert, the commissioner responsible for EU competition policy, to contest the merger between Boeing and McDonnell Douglas in 1997. The commission's intervention to block the merger between two American corporations, overriding the ruling of the U.S. Justice Department's antitrust division that it did not constitute a market-restraining action potentially damaging to consumer interests, threatened to trigger a transatlantic trade war, though U.S. competitors of the merging companies were among the most vociferous plaintiffs.

While the commission initiated the review and throughout was the protagonist on the European side, the French government vigorously backed van Miert's hard line. It holds a large stake in Aérospatiale, which in turn is the largest component of Airbus Industrie, with a Frenchman at its helm. Paris also had been the strongest advocate of an aggressive industrial policy to bolster Airbus's position in its duel with Boeing. Massive financial subsidies from all the Airbus partner governments, along with the underwriting of concessionary financing sales, had put the United States and the Europeans (with France in the lead) at loggerheads for more than a decade. American complaints that Airbus was the beneficiary of public monies that distorted market forces to Boeing's disadvantage were countered by claims that Boeing received indirect government subsidies via R&D support for the development of military aircraft with clear applications to the civilian side of the company. The debate was muted, though not resolved, by the hard-won accord reached in 1994 to limit subsidies and to restrict export financing. From Paris's vantage point, the merger rekindled fears of U.S. government subsidies funneling into Boeing's coffers through McDonnell Douglas's defense sector. American resentment of France's centralized approach in the one industrial sector that had been clearly dominated by America lingered. Paris, for its part, remained dedicated to promoting Airbus. Export earnings, jobs, national prestige, and Europe's full presence in a key sector of technology and industry combined to make Airbus a symbol of French, and European, economic prowess in a high-voltage challenge to American technical supremacy. Van Miert's injection of the commission into this high-stakes contest was a welcome call to arms for the French. By contrast, the official reaction in Washington was a mix of consternation and puzzlement: why were the Europeans going out of their way to pick a fight?[15]

The ensuing struggle was notable for its intensity and compression. In a tense three-month period, the crisis simmered close to the boiling point. The outcome was a clear victory for the EU, for Airbus, and for France. Boeing was forced to make concessions; they included relinquishing control over the replacement parts business for McDonnell Douglas aircraft, rescinding exclusivity contracts with U.S. airlines, and introducing safeguards to prevent Boeing's civilian sector from benefiting from Defense Department R&D funding for McDonnell Douglas's military projects. The interplay among the parties revealed pronounced differences in how the two countries approach international commercial issues. In Paris, the battle was joined eagerly and ardently. French leaders encouraged van Miert, the commission as a whole, and member governments to set stringent conditions for approval of the merger and to resist American pressure for a facile compromise. Their advocacy fell on the receptive ears of the full commission, which backed the principles van Miert represented, and of some other governments sensitive to the issue of defending multinational projects. Airbus thus was the beneficiary of both van Miert's passionate dedication to principles of open competition and the French government's equal passion in championing a company that stood for French and European national prestige and industrial competence.

The Clinton administration, from first to last, had trouble deciding what it could or should do in response to the challenge from Brussels. Entreaties from the Boeing management that it do something to protect the company, and American commercial interests, were sent to the White House.[16] The administration's equivocation had a number of causes. For one thing, it was chary of opening yet another front in its contentious trade disputes with the Europeans, which already were souring transatlantic relations. Moreover, it had viewed competition policy as one area where the sides could work together constructively. Little more than a year earlier, Washington had entered into an understanding with the EU that set the guidelines for creating a joint surveillance mechanism on corporate mergers with a wide authority over commerce in both jurisdictions.[17] It sought to avoid a confrontation that would call into question prospects for so signal an accomplishment. In addition, there was not a strong tradition of close collaboration between the federal government and the great American corporations—outside of the defense field. Boeing and the White House also were slow in realizing that the gray Brussels administrator, Mr. van Miert, was anything but a nonentity. He would fight his side tenaciously with the strong backing of the full commission and at least tacit support from member governments.

Only slowly did the full magnitude of the threat become evident. The Clinton administration never did succeed in formulating a strategy worthy of the name. The dearth of conviction and will within the administration was conveyed by the paltry weaponry it deployed for the supposed battle. The most powerful retaliatory measure it threatened to use was a plan to curtail flights to France—a convenient target not only because France was seen as instigating the EU's hard line, but also because it was at the time one of the few major countries without a full air transport agreement with the United States.[18] The French were more honored than intimidated by being singled out. It was the ideal occasion to raise high the banner of Europe in a contest with the United States where Paris enjoyed sympathy throughout the community. President Chirac and Prime Minister Jospin outdid each other in criticizing the U.S. administration's attempt to link the Boeing affair to the negotiation of a bilateral "Open Skies" agreement that would loosen restrictions on access to each other's civilian aviation market. Moreover, threatening an action that would inconvenience tens of thousands of American tourists at the height of summer holidays lacked credibility. The threat itself, as publicly issued by President Clinton, was contingent on the parties' inability to reach agreement—in effect an encouragement to compromise a less than a stalwart defense of Boeing.

The French relished their position as the foremost opponent of the merger between the two American aircraft manufacturers. The French president encouraged the commission to "defend European interests against attacks that are unacceptable in a free-trade society," thus associating himself with van Miert's genuine devotion to competition in the marketplace. The French clearly were ready to go to the mat over the merger. The commission was solid in its backing of van Miert. However, neither Boeing nor the Clinton administration was similarly prepared for the rough-and-tumble. Amidst growing talk of an impending trade war (mainly on the European side), Boeing threw in the towel by rescinding the exclusivity contracts it had with several airlines to supply all their aircraft for a fixed period. Added to agreements already made on the replacement parts issue as well as that of containing "spillover" of technology from military to civilian aviation, the keystone to a deal was in place. Besides, these concessions notwithstanding, Boeing survived the ordeal with the essence of its merger deal intact.

An inattentive public and distracted Congress gave the president the political space in which to arrange a quiet surrender without firing a serious shot. A story that was on the front pages of European newspapers for weeks on end was largely relegated to the business section of U.S. newspapers. Only at the height of the crisis did it attain the status of a serious news item. Even then, it had far less saliency to American political elites than to their transatlantic counterparts. By contrast, many in France were caught up in what they experienced as a David and Goliath struggle. They reveled at having bested Uncle Sam. The "fight for Airbus" was heralded as a "clear turning point in the relationship between Europe and America." Some were so imbued with war fever as to call for pressing ahead in quest of total victory. France's Edith Cresson, the EU commissioner for research and a former Socialist prime minister, voted against the terms arduously won by van Miert in demanding that Boeing eliminate all of McDonnell Douglas's civil aviation operations. The French government, by contrast, knew a victory when it saw one.

The Boeing affair offers perspective on recurrent elements in the equation of Franco-American relations while drawing attention to how the European factor enters into it. Asymmetries were once again in evidence. The perceived stakes were markedly higher for the French government than for the American one. Differences in political saliency and governmental attentiveness were striking. The U.S. economy's greater depth and diversity made it less vulnerable to developments in the global marketplace—even substantial ones—than individual European countries. U.S. tolerances are concomitantly higher. At the level of intangibles, the French preoccupation with measuring itself against the United States contrasts with the American conceit about its natural superiority—a conceit dented by the formidable Japanese challenge in manufacturing but now largely restored by the dynamism of the U.S. economy that in the 1990s outstripped all rivals.

The intensity of French feeling over the Boeing affair was indicative of how aware the French are of American economic prowess. The signal success that the Airbus consortium had registered by 1997 in establishing itself as a viable competitor of Boeing in world markets had not fully overcome anxiety that the Americans somehow could reverse that trend, especially if Boeing and McDonnell Douglas's resources were amalgamated. Their merger was seen in Paris as the logical outgrowth of the Clinton administration's active encouragement of defense industry consolidations. That was exemplified by the "Long Knives Dinner" hosted in 1993 by Secretary of Defense William Perry, where he bluntly spelled out for defense industry leaders why their interests and that of the United States dictated a drastic restructuring. Not unreasonably, therefore, the French expected the Clinton administration to throw its weight behind Boeing, upping the stakes in its contest with the EU Commission. In such a game the American powerhouse had what the military strategists call escalation dominance. Fears of American prowess were somewhat exaggerated by the French transposing onto Washington their own economic philosophy and governmental method. If Jacques Chirac or Lionel Jospin had been in Bill Clinton's place, he would have mobilized state and corporate powers to maintain Boeing's supremacy in defense of the national interest. That the French Colbertian tradition is decidedly non-American and that business and government work comfortably hand in hand only in the defense sector and airspace is recognized intellectually. But that knowledge does not always lead to dispassionate assessment of American policy. Moreover, the Clinton administration's rhetoric about its commitment to promoting jobs for Americans, along with a sporadic resort to unilateral measures, gave credence to impressions that the U.S. government was ready to step into the arena to back Boeing. Under the Clinton administration, the gap between American rhetoric (consistently intransigent) and American action (mostly tempered and conciliatory) was visible to the eye of the detached beholder. On the other hand, the vast increases in defense spending initially planned by the George W. Bush administration, reinforced in the aftermath of September 11, 2001, strengthened in France and Europe the impression that the U.S. government uses defense spending to support the civil aircraft industry.

The other lesson to be drawn from the Boeing affair is that the EU acts as a shock absorber between Washington and Paris. Commissioner van Miert, and later the commission as a whole, was the Clinton administration's protagonist. The clash of French and American interests was evident, but the deleterious effects on the overall relationship were mitigated. The commission's intervention to block the proposed General Electric–Honeywell merger four years later regenerated tensions between Brussels and Washington. The French government was not a significant player in this affair, though it fully backed the authority and judgment of van Miert's successor, Mario Monti. The EU ruling did aggravate relations with the Bush administration, which, like Congress, is hesitant to put external constraints on the American free-market economy. In particular, it had the side

effect of heightening strains over the "foreign sales corporation" tax concession issue. The EU's possible imposition of $4 billion of sanctions on
American exports if the WTO were to find the United States in continuing
noncompliance with its interim ruling had been dubbed "a nuclear device"
by Robert Zoellick, the U.S. trade representative, with the promise of retali-
ation. The French pedigree of his EU counterpart, Pascal Lamy, associates
France (in some American minds) with any aggressive EU challenge to the
United States on commercial issues.[19] In this respect, the European Union's
governing strength and assertiveness can have a negative spillover effect on
French-American relations when the French government keeps a low profile on a contentious issue.

U.S. Triumphalism

French apprehensions about the United States' increasing aggressiveness in
the trade field are fed by the triumphal tone in the public pronouncements
of U.S. leaders. The stellar performance of the American economy throughout the 1990s—bolstered by steadily rising stock values—contrasted sharply
with Western Europe's struggle against high unemployment and sluggish
growth (let alone Japan's prolonged recession). It had restored the twin articles of faith that the United States had regained its natural position as the
world's strongest economy and had found the formula for success in the era
of globalization that others should apply. American triumphalism seemed
justified by its performance and by the supposedly superior liberal economic philosophy that it demonstrated. The old impulse to instruct the rest
of the world in the lessons learned from American success reemerged with
renewed conviction. Understatement and self-doubt have never been
American national traits. The exuberance of the Clinton administration
created a self-congratulatory mood. Advertising its achievements by contrasting them with the weaker performance of other industrial countries
also served the domestic political end of reminding people that American
prosperity was not a general phenomenon; rather, it owed it to the wisdom
and skill of administration policymakers.

    This newfound triumphalism was on vivid display during the G-7 sum-
mit held in Denver in mid-June 1997—just as van Miert's challenge to Boeing was cresting. It was used by the Clinton team as a platform to propagate
the United States' creed for contending with the forces of globalization
while lowering the public debt and bolstering employment. Lawrence
Summers, then undersecretary of the Treasury for international affairs, set

the tone in a declaration clearly aimed at the visiting foreign leaders: "The United States today is in an extremely strong position. We are the only military superpower. It is becoming evident that we also are the only economic superpower. We dominate virtually all of the sectors of the post-industrial economy. . . . There is a unique chance to shape the world in our manner."[20] In staking a claim to "the economic truth" and promoting American methods, U.S. officials did not stint on giving advice to their European counterparts. Solicited or not, the United States conducted a tutorial on how to manage a modern-day economy. Secretary of the Treasury Robert Rubin was particularly blunt in his discussion with the new French finance minister, Dominique Strauss-Kahn. Rubin made a point of critiquing the Jospin government's controversial proposal to cut the work week from thirty-nine to thirty-five hours (at no pay reduction), a plan officially aimed at thinning the ranks of the unemployed, a sensitive domestic political issue. Rubin buttressed his argument with pointed reference to workers at a Jeep factory in Ohio who, in order to save their jobs, agreed to work up to fifty-four hours a week with overtime.

There could be no better example of how the American model of bottom-line capitalism reinforced the discomfort of the newly elected French government. Americans looked all too ready to subordinate the welfare of workers to the god of global competitiveness, an approach that in practice had contributed to nearly stagnant real wages for the average American worker for a quarter of a century while creating the widest income disparities in the developed world. The new Socialist government in Paris was dedicated to finding a way out of France's unemployment dilemma (shared with most of Western Europe) without squeezing workers' wages and denying them their hard-won, much appreciated safeguards against arbitrary acts of management. Indeed, on these and related issues of social welfare, and although they are highly critical of the thirty-five-hour week, Jacques Chirac and a majority of conservative French politicians were to the left of the Clinton administration. Chirac was as exercised by the American tutorial in liberal economics as the Socialists were. The Denver celebration of U.S. superiority he found "too much."[21] In Paris, Lionel Jospin was more blunt, denouncing before the National Assembly "a certain tendency toward hegemony in the United States." Defending the social market economy, he declared that "Europe does not have the same model as the United States, it has always tried to preserve a balance between economic efficiency and social welfare."[22] Jospin bristled at American disparagement of his program, as typified by a *Newsweek* story that asked whether the victory of the French

Socialists was "the foresign of a revolt" against American liberalism or "the last spasm of a French resistance to reform of the providential state."[23] The French impression of the United States' arrogance could not be easily shrugged off as characteristic American enthusiasm and ignorance of the sensitivities of the rest of the world.[24]

By the end of the 1990s, strident talk of economic war had faded in both Paris and Washington. American officials, realizing how counterproductive it was to trumpet American success, lowered the volume at which they broadcast their message. Instead, they concentrated on problem solving—whether the problem was disputes with the EU on compliance with WTO rulings, the issue of extraterritorial sanctions, or restarting the Millennium Round of trade negotiations. The U.S. interest in European prosperity and stability could not be advanced by hectoring lectures from across the Atlantic. For French leaders, the logic of pragmatism spread from the security sphere into the economic sphere. Prime Minister Jospin, encouraged by his finance minister, overcame his reflexive rejection of American economic thinking to appreciate that there was some virtue, and relevance, to the American experience in job creation. His acknowledgment in an address to the National Press Club in June 1998 that there were things worthy of emulation in the U.S. experience signaled an end to ideological combat, though significant differences of outlook and priority remained. Jospin's late-dawning awareness that U.S. growth had created real rather than dummy jobs was revealing of how little even many top politicians know about the United States.[25]

Stereotypes sometimes contain some kernel of truth. The American faith in free markets is deep seated, as is French belief in the stabilizing hand of the state. The election of George W. Bush in 2000 revived French images of an America devoted to unbridled capitalism. Public declarations by Treasury Secretary Paul O'Neill that the United States henceforth would take a hands-off approach to global problems rekindled fears in Paris that Washington might be less than a full player in multilateral management of the world economy. Expressing skepticism about the efficacy of IMF-organized intervention in financial markets to deal with monetary crises, he placed more stock in self-equilibrating markets if they were not distorted by governmental interference. Keeping markets informed and unfettered could, he averred, preempt financial crises. O'Neill voiced similar doubts about the value of meetings among finance ministers of the Group of 7 industrialized nations (the so-called G-7) and the type of informal concert they exercised.[26]

These remarks sounded a dissonant note in French ears and were taken as signs of an American reversion from structured multilateralism in the economic domain that was a piece of the new administration's seeming disparagement of major components of the international arms control regime. There was an element of irony in France's anxieties about the United States distancing itself from an IMF that too often in the past seemed a pliable instrument of American policy. U.S. exceptionality could take various forms, but was always troubling. The challenge of harnessing American power and influence to a collective process wherein France exercised a substantial measure of influence—on its own or, increasingly, via Europe—remained a constant. The Bush administration's gradual demonstration that it would continue to be a constructive player in multilateral forums left unanswered the key question, for France, of the terms of that engagement.

Europe Redux

Unaltered was the French assessment that building Europe was essential to a French strategy for dealing with the twin challenges of globalization and the United States' hegemonic power—a reality whether it was driven by overweening national ambition or not. The enhanced Europe of Maastricht and the European Central Bank (ECB) is visualized as an economic entity capable of channeling the dynamic forces of the global economy and ensuring that policies for fixing its structural problems will not be dictated by the United States. By readying itself to do so, the EU meets French needs. The governments of the other fourteen members have made the same judgment. Logically that means that their national needs are convergent. In the abstract, that is true. Implicit in EU construction is the premise of the obsolescence of the old game of amassing economic assets to increase the power of states in contention with each other. It is the plus-sum game of interdependence following the rules of market competition that prevails. Less self-evident is what variation of open-market capitalism will prevail. Appreciable differences do exist among the fifteen, even if there is no apostle of the American brand of freewheeling capitalism. Of course, Tony Blair's government has markedly different views from most continental governments on how much government regulation of the marketplace is compatible with growth and efficiency. And certainly there have been clear disagreements within the EU Commission and among national governments on whether the EU should be an unalloyed proponent of fully liberalizing the international trade regime.

For France, these issues are of cardinal importance. The minimalist liberal state, with a narrowly construed role in economic management, remains an alien concept to nearly all of the French political class. It is true that there has been a progressive scaling back of the state's role in France. Incrementally, by degrees, Socialists and Gaullists alike have found it prudent, and necessary, to abandon cherished ideas about the dirigiste state. François Mitterrand learned the painful lesson in the early 1980s that even the mildest version of socialism in one country was an impossibility (his early nationalizations aside). His adherence to the *franc fort* policy, dictated by a combination of strategic monetary and political reasons, required that macroeconomic management observe orthodox liberal norms. Statist thinking about public ownership has changed more slowly. The once large galaxy of publicly opened enterprises has dwindled considerably, though. First a series of conservative governments, willingly, and then the Socialist government of Lionel Jospin, *contre-coeur*, have yielded to the logic of privatization.[27] More broadly, the logic of national self-sufficiency is at odds with the logic of cross-national European alliances as the most efficacious way to maintain a critical mass of technological and financial assets and avoid dependence on U.S. corporations. The outlook and attitude of the dirigiste state survive in another respect. It is an article of belief that national competitive advantage is a product of national policies over time. In the French conception, that means not only sound fiscal and monetary policies but also an enlightened industrial policy. This is especially true where financial viability and product development require the application of sophisticated technology and very large capital infusions. The Airbus project is the outstanding example. French governments, Gaullist or Socialist, to varying degrees are reluctant to abandon completely the state's interest in key fields like communications, even as they transform state monopolies into publicly held companies. France's retention of "golden shares," which give the state a veto over merger or acquisition with foreign firms, brings France into conflict with its more liberal-minded trading partners. The admission by Finance Minister Dominique Strauss-Kahn in 1998 that the government stood ready to use its golden shares in Elf Aquitaine to protect it from acquisitive Anglo-Saxon companies exemplified the continued perceived threat to French national interests by the predatory behavior of aggressive American business firms (now a contagion spreading to French companies, too). Ironically, in the Elf case, Paris found itself under attack by a coalition of the U.S. government and the EU Commission. Competition commissioner Mario Monti, following on the initiative of his predecessor, Karel van Miert, has instituted a proceeding against France in the European Court of Justice over the state's exercise of its golden share prerogatives to keep newly privatized companies from becoming the prey of foreign bidders. The EU Commission, France's ally in the fight over the Boeing–McDonnell Douglas merger, became its foe. This was not a case of a role reversal for the commission. Rather it was a demonstration that the commission's exercise of its mandate sometimes conforms to French aspirations that "Europe" be a force multiplier of French interests; at other times it constitutes a threat to France's self-defined economic security. Supranational authorities may not be as uncontrollable as markets, but they are themselves symptomatic of how risky is France's bet on "Europe" as a counter to Americanization of the global economy.

The appointment of Pascal Lamy to replace Sir Leon Brittan as trade commissioner in 1999 made a Frenchman the EU's standard-bearer in dealing with the United States on commercial issues. Lamy, chef de cabinet for Jacques Delors at the EU Commission during the critical years of designing plans for the single market and launching the Maastricht enterprise, has belied any suspicion that he would strongly favor the French position on contentious transatlantic trade issues. At the same time, it is by no means obvious that he can use his position and status in French political circles to reconcile Paris with the inescapable realities of free trade. His appointment does ensure two things: French concerns and sensitivities are acknowledged in Brussels; and Americans' innate suspicion of France's mercantilism and anti-American tendencies still find ready reason to approach dealings with the EU with caution.

The buildup of festering trade disputes ensures that economic dealings will be an aggravating factor in French-American relations. Rancorous issues such as restrictions on access to the EU market for beef raised on hormone additives, the running controversy over genetically modified foodstuffs, and the seemingly endless banana war that was solved in a mere few weeks by a determined effort on the part of U.S. Trade Representative Robert Zoellick and European Trade Commissioner Pascal Lamy are typified as much by divergent cultural attitudes as by conflicts of commercial interest. France has been in the thick of the fray. It argues strenuously that differing social norms and practices are valid considerations in determining the limits of the state's right to regulate trade in foodstuffs. Popular aversion to modified, "unnatural" agricultural produce (publicized in theatrical campaigns that join mavericks like José Bové with farmers' associations) creates political incentives for French officials to resist the mechanical application of WTO rules. The United States, for its part, sees both the law and science as being on its side, though it is far from blameless in implementing WTO decisions. It interprets other countries' refusal to comply with WTO rulings, or attempts to neutralize those rulings by stigmatizing questionable imports, as outright violations of free-trade principles and the law. The ensuing conflict, which mixes issues of the WTO's authority, globalization imagery and fears, an assertive EU, and a righteous United States, is not readily susceptible to the pragmatic problem-solving approach of Pascal Lamy and Robert Zoellick. For Washington and Paris, the common challenge is to contain without ignoring the passions and politics of the globalization scare while doing the hard bargaining that serves their national interests.

Economic and Monetary Union

The building of an Economic and Monetary Union (EMU) in 1999 as a second pillar of the EU was a landmark achievement. Historians are likely to view it as a turning point in the Euro-American relationship as well. If the profound potential of EMU is realized, much of the credit will rest with France. Successive French governments fostered the idea, forged a partnership with Germany to promote it, provided the political impetus to incorporate it into the Single European Act of 1986, elaborated the intellectual justification for the single currency, and seized the opportunity presented by Chancellor Kohl to make the euro the symbol of a post–cold war Europe of political harmony and economic harmonization. Frenchmen critically placed in the EU administration, led by Jacques Delors, were EMU's escort guard.[28]

The saga of EMU, as related from the French perspective, has three interwoven themes: influence, jobs, and competitiveness. The great issues related to securing France's place as an influential power in world affairs are intermixed with the bread-and-butter issues of jobs and marketplace competitiveness. The country struggles to find an answer to the forces of the modern world economy that minimizes vulnerability without giving up distinctive French traditions and methods. A unified Europe is the French answer to neutralizing Germany's rising power and to countervailing the dominant power of the United States. Jacques Delors, president of the EU Commission in the late 1980s, expressed the views of his compatriots in seeing its creation as the best way to extend France's influence in a community more and more dominated by the mark. Yet Europe itself diminishes France's control of its own affairs. There is the rub.

France's conception of EMU is two-dimensional. It is at once a defensive measure as regards the United States, Germany, and the financial markets and a means to increase its leverage on all of the forces reshaping the world economy. It thus epitomizes the mingling of ambition and insecurity in French foreign policy. Together they create a powerful situational logic that has sustained a national strategy committed to monetary integration since the early 1970s. It should not be forgotten that the origins of monetary union can found in the thinking of Gaullist president Georges Pompidou. That thinking led to the European summit in the Hague in 1969, which defined the project along the lines it eventually took. The exception was the brief period between 1981 and 1983 when the newly elected President Mitterrand (with Delors as his economics and finance minister) sought vainly to follow an expansionary policy before abandoning the effort in the face of mounting deficits and after three devaluations of the franc. The penalties imposed on the French economy by the currency exchanges convinced the president that fulfilling his progressive economic and social program was conditioned on France's adherence to strict budgetary and monetary discipline. Mitterrand, most of his Socialist followers, and the country as a whole learned three lessons: (1) the notion of an independent national economic policy in the era of European integration and global competition was an illusion; (2) France was obliged to follow a sound money policy that emulated Germany's because of the greater weight of the German economy and the greater strength of the deutsche mark; and (3) the only alternative to letting the Bundesbank act as a de facto central bank for the EU zone was to Europeanize it. The last became an unswerving French objective.

French leaders were prepared to take austerity measures that would confirm France's readiness to be as financially virtuous as their neighbors across the Rhine. The *franc fort* policy of shadowing the mark was observed with remarkable consistency by left and right governments alike—in periods of "cohabitation" as well as under unified executives. The price paid in slow growth and high unemployment was considerable. Although a number of factors came together to produce a sluggish economy, primary among them was the need to match the Bundesbank's tight money policy and the budgetary restraint dictated by the strict "convergence criteria" by which candidates for joining EMU were measured. The former was particularly irksome because the Bundesbank's high interest rate policy was the result of

Chancellor Kohl's decision to debt-finance the huge costs of union with the East, including valuation of the East German mark at parity with the deutsche mark. The effect that a political decision in Bonn could have on economic management throughout the EU was a compelling validation of why EMU had to happen. The French government found itself accused of following a monetary policy so restrictive that it had a deflationary impact on the economy, when in fact it was not the *franc fort* but repercussions of German unification that were the culprit.

The monetary union now is an accomplished fact, albeit one whose full impact on the continent's economic structures and world monetary affairs will take years to register. French leaders, for their part, have never hidden their hope that EMU would tilt the transatlantic scales toward Europe. As President Chirac had asserted on numerous occasions: "We have a need for a dynamic European entity that can only be European, in whose service it is necessary to have a money capable of resisting the pressures of the dollar and capable of competing against the dollar on equal terms."[29] French unhappiness with the dollar's domination of international finance has deep roots, as does its discontent with American dominance in the security field. Charles de Gaulle inveighed against the extravagant privilege that the United States enjoyed thanks to the dollar's wide acceptance as an exchange and reserve currency. His policy of systematically cashing in dollars at the U.S. Treasury's gold window was both a symbolic and a tangible way of protesting the United States' self-indulgence in covering its rising balance-of-trade deficits by printing money—that is, dollars that much of the world was willing to hold.

The turbulence of international monetary affairs in the 1970s that brought down the Bretton Woods system heightened French concerns about the disequilibrating and disruptive effects of a dollar-dominated monetary regime. A series of shocks—beginning with the Nixon administration's sudden unilateral decision to end the dollar's convertibility (literally closing the gold window), the decision not to defend the dollar's fixed value against other currencies that led to a generalized system of floating exchange rates, the oil embargoes and subsequent price hikes that set off an inflationary spiral, and then, mounting third world indebtedness and the accelerated petro-dollar recycling that sustained it—together made a powerful case for France to seek a measure of order, and control, by linking the franc to other European currencies.

The rekindled move toward monetary union in the mid-1980s was largely of French inspiration. One negative reference point was the volatility in the dollar's value (which doubled and then was halved again within a decade). France had been especially sensitive to how a volatile dollar affects the terms of trade. Two other features of the dollar's privileged position may be curtailed by EMU. One is the disproportionate share of securities offerings worldwide that are denominated in dollars, a state of affairs that redounds to the advantage of American financial houses. The other is the influence that the United States wields over international monetary policy—an influence that is disproportionate to the size of the American economy or the strength of its financial institutions but is commensurate with the pivotal role of the dollar in global finance. The hope in Paris is that over time (but preferably sooner rather than later) the dollar's dethronement will result in a more equitable sharing of financial power with the EU, and perhaps Japan, while strengthening Europe's hands in multilateral monetary negotiations.

Whether French expectations for EMU are fulfilled depends on a number of problematic elements. One can reasonably conclude that monetary union is now an irreversible fact of life and that the euro has all the features that are identified by economic theory and by history as characteristic of an international currency.[30] However, the path is strewn with obstacles, both technical and political. Institutionally, there are two anomalies that complicate the formulation and implementation of a one-size-fits-all monetary policy for the twelve member countries that have relinquished authority to the European Central Bank. The first arises from the discrepancy between monetary union and the diversity of economic conditions. Differentials of national economic performance—due in part to differences in budgetary, tax, and social policies—ensure that any course set by the ECB in Frankfurt will be less than optimal (indeed at times unhealthy) for some.

The second anomaly is that EMU has created a central bank with a high degree of autonomy without creating an analogous political authority with which it cooperates or to which it is accountable. By treaty, the ECB is accountable to the Council of Ministers. Modeled on the Bundesbank, though, its articles of incorporation endow it with a high degree of independence and a mandate that gives priority to price stability. The bank has set an annual inflation rate of 2 percent as the ceiling for maintaining price stability. France has led moves to place the ECB under some form of political constraint. To Paris's way of thinking, the notion of an autonomous ECB determining the political fate of Europeans is unsettling because it is at once uncontrollable and predictable. That is to say, it is a facsimile of the Deutsche Bundesbank in constitution and mandate at the European level;

thus it lacks the implicit restraints of its prototype, which—for all its vaunted independence—operated within a fully developed political context to which it could not be oblivious. The ECB will be freer to set a monetarist course for the monetary union that conforms fully to the precepts of its strict constructionist monetarism. The irony is that the ECB's image as the ultimate technocracy should haunt the French government, which is characterized by a fusion of political and technical elites. They have perfected technocratic methods within the EU Commission in ways that have nicely served French national interests.[31]

The weaker the oversight powers of the Council of Ministers, the less constraining its political influence and the greater the certainty that a devoutly orthodox ECB will adhere to tight money policies. As far as Paris is concerned, whether that is the right policy cannot be answered by monetarist textbooks. Instead, the criterion of price stability should take into account social costs—and their political consequences. The latter point is unspoken but no less a concern for that. France acknowledged the principle of an independent central bank through legislation passed in 1993 and 1998 that appreciably loosened the link between the executive and the bank. That action, though, expressed the imperative of preparing for the joint move toward monetary union as much as it did belief in the unmitigated virtue of central bank autonomy.

Official American support for EMU has been unwavering. Steadfast backing for the euro project from successive American administrations is in contrast with the pronounced skepticism among a significant and vocal segment of the economic fraternity. Doubts as to the EMU's desirability, workability, and political purpose have been heard most often from orthodox economic liberals.[32] Broadcast in a variety of international forums, these doubts have raised hackles in many European capitals, above all Paris. As thin skinned as ever about American criticism of their favored ideas, French officials interpret the intellectual assault on EMU as motivated by a combination of intellectual hubris and political ill will. In some quarters, it was taken to be the true voice of American opinion that could not bear the loss of dollar supremacy that the euro's launch presages. There is a kernel of truth to that accusation: high-powered American academics' estimations of the degree of influence possible or desirable for satisfying tangible national interests often exceed the more realistic and qualified expectations of American officials. The latter view conforms to the support that the United States has given the Maastricht project as a whole.[33] The reasons are strategic. A united, prosperous, and self-confident European Union is seen as a powerfully stabilizing force in postcommunist Europe. Monetary union contributes to that end by facilitating growth, interring the nationalist ghosts of the past stirred up by German unification, and raising the stakes that member states have in a peaceful undivided continent. Moreover, a deepening EU is taken to be compatible with retaining NATO as the West's primary security body and with the two organizations' complementary rather than competitive enlargement. Furthermore, in the global economic perspective the boost that EMU is expected to give Western European economies eases the burden on the United States to be the engine of growth for the world economy.

As for the euro's possible challenge to dollar supremacy, Washington took a generally relaxed attitude toward that prospect throughout the 1990s. It was due in good part to the extraordinary strength of the U.S. economy. The combination of robust growth and sound fundamentals (such as a budget surplus and low inflation) instilled confidence that the dollar would remain attractive as an investment instrument and an asset holding. It is accepted that the euro gradually will acquire a place in international finance that will reduce the dollar's dominant position. But that long-term prospect to date has caused few worries. Optimism that macroeconomic management in the United States will continue to be prudent, and economic performance commensurately positive, encourages the belief that there is no reason to fear a dramatic or quick drop in the influence the United States exerts on world monetary matters.

The virtuous circle of a strong economy sustaining a strong dollar could reverse itself. The danger is that a slowing economy would attract fewer offshore dollars, lowering the dollar's exchange rate and generating further downward pressures on inflated equity prices. The euro's acceptance as an alternative to the dollar would add to downward pressures on the exchange market and accentuate the greenback's weakness. The sharp downturn in the U.S. economy in the second half of 2001 did not set such a train in action, to the puzzlement of many economic analysts. At what point, and by what combination of objective economic factors, loose fiscal policy, and market psychology such a downward spiral could be set in motion is unpredictable. The consequences, however, are foreseeable.

One, trade conflicts will sharpen, for it would no longer be possible to finance the trade deficit cheaply by drawing in dollars without raising interest rates. Pressures to bolster exports will mount. Stress would be placed on those sectors where the potential for expanded markets overseas is greatest: in agriculture and high-technology products. These are exactly the sectors that have become the main commercial battleground between the United States and the EU. France, given its own stakes in both and its position as the most visible advocate of taking a tough line with the Americans, would be in the thick of the fight. However predictable the exchanges between Washington and Paris, this is not an instance of *"plus ça change . . . "* Battles over agricultural products, including hormone additives in beef and genetically engineered foodstuffs, will be hard fought. No American administration has the political luxury of sacrificing the interests of American farmers for the sake of consensus on a larger package of trade agreements. This logic holds even if mounting current account deficits do not send the U.S. economy into a tailspin. Exports are crucial to the health of the nation's farm economy. Nearly a quarter of all production is sold abroad (creating 750,000 jobs). Exports have declined substantially since they reached record levels of $60 billion in 1996. Telecommunications, civilian aircraft, and an array of technology-based service industries will also become objects of a high-pressure U.S. campaign to unblock European markets. The Bush administration is showing that it will take a hard-nosed approach to trade negotiations. For its part, France's residual mercantilist instinct to protect national champions in the name of economic security ensures that the line of tension between the two countries will not slacken.

A heightened contest for monetary influence between the United States and the EU will be the other likely consequence of a serious deterioration in the strength of the dollar and the American economy. The issues will vary, as will the scope and intensity of differences, depending on exact circumstances. The struggle for the upper hand in what overall will remain a collective enterprise that serves both parties' interest will be conducted decorously. It will be a contest of ideas more than of interests, with ideas being the currency of status and influence. It is a game that the French relish and are adept at. They will play it in their national capacity as a member of the IMF's Interim Committee, at G-8 meetings, as a major player on the Euro-12 committee (consisting of the twelve countries participating in EMU), through the representative of the Banque de France on the ECB's board of directors, and—in principle—through the bank presidency beginning in 2002.[34] The French line of thinking on outstanding issues of world monetary management often will run counter to the United States' position: on the value and means of capital flows, on oversight of financial markets, on the ground rules of IMF emergency assistance in national monetary crises, on IMF decisionmaking arrangements, on maintaining stability of currency values on the exchange markets. On all of these questions, the French philosophical and political bias places less confidence in the self-equilibrating capacity of markets and more in the potential benefits of state authorities structuring and managing them. As Prime Minister Jospin has declared: "We do not resist globalization. We want to civilize it."[35]

With the end of the renewed American hegemony over world monetary affairs—an outcome that is as inevitable as the timing is unpredictable—the form of the French challenge to the United States will change. Gradually, the self-styled mission of imposing restraints on the American Gulliver will give way to setting the terms of a more equal partnership between the United States and Europe. How Europe identifies itself and what guides its external policies will go far to shape the Franco-American relationship. France's place at the European table, in turn, will go far toward shaping the wider Euro-American relationship.

The prospect of economic and monetary union has exposed some raw feelings on both sides of the Atlantic. Some French officials have harbored suspicions that the United States wants the project to fail, public pronouncements to the contrary notwithstanding. Financial interests, supposedly in league with U.S. officials, allegedly fear the emergence of a rival to dollar dominance with the advantages of U.S. financial houses vitiated. These suspicions were aroused when the Exchange Rate Mechanism (ERM) came unstuck in the crises of 1992 and 1993. The former jeopardized ratification of the Maastricht Treaty; the latter put in doubt whether member states would meet the deadlines for achieving monetary union. Jacques Delors was among those who spoke darkly of an "Anglo-Saxon" conspiracy to undermine confidence in the viability of the ERM. The 1992 crisis that saw the withdrawal of sterling and the Italian lira, forced by waves of selling on the exchange markets, evoked angry attacks on speculators who supposedly acted as de facto agents of those who wanted the EMU project to fail. George Soros, the Hungarian-born and New York–based financier who supposedly pocketed a multibillion-dollar profit from leading the speculative charge against sterling, was the lightning rod for these accusations of an Anglo-Saxon conspiracy. His dubious qualifications for the role did not prevent his being so cast.

There is a current of sentiment in some French circles that the United States and Britain are allied in a broad strategy aimed at thwarting European (and thereby French) ambitions while keeping France on the margins of international power. But fortunately, it is on the wane. A younger generation of leaders, less in thrall to history and more cosmopolitan in their experience, do not share the instincts of some members of the older generation.

They know the United States better and recognize its contradictions and ambivalence about its world role; they understand the workings of impersonal international markets; and they seek ways to reconcile French identity and national interest with the complexities and opportunities of a world that in some respects is of American making and congenial to the United States. For their part, French entrepreneurs, financiers, and managers are a significant presence in the transnational economy. Witness that France is now the world's third largest exporter of services and third largest source of foreign investment.

A matching prejudice has been evident in Washington among the less cosmopolitan figures on the public scene who bedevil globally oriented officials. A key factor in setting the tone for new forms of power sharing on monetary matters will be the U.S. Congress. Congress's readiness to vent its ingrained distrust of the IMF could grow commensurate with the rise in influence of other governments over the fund's business. A president who can manage diplomacy simultaneously on two fronts—the domestic and the multinational—and is ready to make heavy investments of political capital in each will be necessary to prevent parochial American attitudes from upsetting what in any event will be delicate relationships. Stereotyping of France (and of Europe generally) and a denigration of their ambitions is evident on Capitol Hill. It was epitomized in 1999 by Senate majority leader Trent Lott in resisting the appropriation of the $18 billion pledged by the Clinton administration to an expanded IMF loan facility. He declared himself opposed to giving American taxpayers' dollars to an organization run by a "French socialist" who would waste it on undeserving foreign governments.[36] It provoked mirth in France to see the straitlaced Michel Camdessus labeled a "socialist" when he is a typically apolitical civil servant. The negative connotations of *IMF, French,* and *socialist* are potent in some U.S. political circles, particularly when used together in one sentence. The existence of such attitudes at high political levels gives pause to the French as they contemplate doing business with a government that must operate in so parochial a political environment.

One further effect of EMU is foreseeable. It will intensify transactions among member governments. The stakes of interactions among governments and with the EU Commission have risen, the demands on policymakers increased. The opportunities as well as the incentives for linkage strategies have expanded. The Euro-12 committee will be a focal point for attempts at influencing ECB policy and most certainly for determining compliance with the provisions of the 1997 Growth and Stability Pact. This agreement, finalized at the EU Council meetings in Amsterdam, is designed to foster the coordination of economic policies, strengthen the conditions for price stability and sustainable growth, and provide stringent limits to budgetary positions. Given the leeway that exists for interpretation and application of those provisions, bargaining is inevitable. What governments bring to the table need not be limited to matters immediately germane to the consideration at hand. Matters outside the EU ambit could be brought into play, tacitly if not explicitly. The nature and frequency of such linkages are unknowable. So, too, is how they might bear on American dealings with EU governments and the community as a whole. The situational logic suggests, though, that the locus for collective Western action has shifted. For those who would limit and channel U.S. influence, like France, the prospect is favorable.

The Defense Industry

Commercial rivalry between the United States and France extends to arms exports. It is a competition made acute by the rising costs of high-tech weaponry at a time of stagnant defense budgets and constricted markets. The shifting terms of that competition reveal the interplay between the forces that are reshaping the two countries' security and economic relationship: American global dominance based in large part on its technological leadership; French dedication to maintaining national and European autonomy while resisting the perceived American drive toward hegemony; the Western Europeans' newfound commitment to a common foreign and security policy with, as its leitmotiv, a reduction of the capability gap with the United States; and Paris's striving for a strategy that simultaneously leverages its influence within the EU and promotes national ambitions.

France's defense industry bridges the domains of commerce and security. As on all consequential matters of public policy, there are distinct national characteristics rooted in history and tradition. For most of France's history, the French defense industry has been seen by the general public, as well as by the state authorities, as a major national asset. This attitude continues well into the post–cold war period for a combination of reasons: the lessons learned from recent history, a national predilection for technological innovation, and the active role played by the French state in managing the national economy.[37]

The French state has had a central role in mobilizing and deploying economic resources since the seventeenth century, when *colbertisme*, named after a minister of Louis XIV, started to inspire political and industrial leaders, giving the state a major role in industrial development. The French Revolution's centralization had pursued this movement, which was then enshrined in legal codes and administrative rules by Napoléon Bonaparte. The concentration of national energy by the state therefore seemed only natural. After being defeated and occupied by the Germans in an ignominious military defeat in 1940 (*l'abîme*), it is hardly surprising that the French became preoccupied after their liberation with avoiding the repetition of such disasters.[38] French governments after 1945 were determined to achieve a greater measure of self-sufficiency in arms than they had had in the past. This was true under the Fourth Republic, however weak and unstable its many governments might have been. It became a central preoccupation of the state under the Fifth Republic as the quest for a national nuclear military capability dominated the Gaullist defense policy, making technological innovation and capability into central tenets of national policy. Bona fide representatives of the military-industrial complex, such as Pierre Guillaumat under de Gaulle and André Giraud in Valéry Giscard d'Estaing's administration and later, as defense minister, in Jacques Chirac's cohabitation government of 1986–88, participated in French governments.[39] Although François Mitterrand was reluctant at first to be publicly associated with the arms industry, and though in his 1981 presidential election platform he had advocated a reduction in the arms export drive in this sector, his administrations were in fact every way as supportive of the sector as conservative administrations before and since. In the same way, Lionel Jospin's advocacy during the 1997 election campaign of a more "ethical" foreign policy and his government's support in principle for Tony Blair and Robin Cook's "European code of conduct" restricting arms exports have not altered the attitudes of the French state toward either the importance of a defense industry or the need to sustain it through a healthy export capability.

Also and equally important, state support for the armaments industry is institutionalized, with a distinct place in the very structure of the civil service. Thus there is a strict separation, within the Defense Ministry, between a separate and largely autonomous corps of military engineers and the armed forces' regular services. The *ingénieurs de l'armement*, with responsibility for developing the French arms industry, are gathered under the traditionally powerful Délégation Générale pour l'Armement (DGA), which has remarkable control over defense corporations, with much intermingling of personnel.[40] In 1995 the government made the conscious decision to appoint a non-*ingénieur de l'armement*, Jean-Yves Helmer, and gave him a mandate to reduce costs by 30 percent. This attempt to bring the Corps de l'Armement into line was only partly successful, however, and Helmer's successor, Yves Gleizes, appointed in 2001, has spent his whole career in the corps. Decisions in the armaments sector are prepared and often made within this corps, whereas the influence of the services—the main consumers of armaments—is rather limited. In recent times, the reluctance of the Armée de l'Air (the air force) to accept the expensive Rafale aircraft bears witness to the limits of the forces' ability to influence procurement decisions. This reluctance was voiced more or less discreetly by successive chiefs of the air staff, most recently and most vocally in 1996 and 1999 by then chief of the air staff, Air Marshall Jean Rannou.[41]

Both publicly and privately owned firms in the armaments sector were, and still are to a great extent, run by those state-trained *ingénieurs de l'armement*, who are graduates of the elite Ecole Polytechnique and also trained at the Ecole Nationale Supérieure de l'Armement (and for the highfliers among them at midcareer at the Centre des Hautes Etudes de l'Armement [CHEAR]). They are imbued with a strong esprit de corps and convinced of two things: that the fate of the nation's armaments industry and indeed of France's armaments lies in their hands and that technical criteria should generally prevail over operational and financial ones. The *ingénieurs de l'armement* control a specific sector of the French state, with direct supervision over an important branch of French industry; it has no external appointments process (*tour extérieur*) and, as such, it is a body without any real equivalent within the French civil service. Hence a remarkable amount of cohesion characterizes the armaments sector. It is accompanied by a rather defensive attitude toward external influences, especially those from foreign countries, and in particular from France's main competitor and model in the field of armaments since 1945, the United States.

The centralized decisionmaking that comes with such control by a small number of people was very much in keeping with the spirit of the postwar period, when a vast nationalization of industrial assets was deemed essential to reconstructing the French economy and reestablishing the country's stature in the world. The Socialist-inspired nationalization of a large part of the defense industry after World War II was therefore accepted by the French body politic, including the Gaullists. Indeed the domination of advanced technological developments by the French state extended well into the private sector. Dassault, for example, was largely run by military engineers long before its nationalization by the Socialists in 1982 and has continued to be since its return to the private sector in 1987. Aérospatiale is also largely dominated by engineers trained at Polytechnique, and the armaments corps is strongly represented at all levels of the company. The recent amalgamation in 1999 of these two corporations with Matra Hautes Technologies into a new company, Matra-Aérospatiale, which in turn owns 46 percent of Dassault Aviation, might involve some evolution in this respect, though Matra itself is no stranger to the armaments corps. The new company will therefore probably also largely be run by engineers with the same background.

It is not always understood outside its own borders that France has a long tradition of technological prowess, evidenced in its prominent role since the early days of the aircraft and automotive industries. France is not only and certainly no longer principally a nation of farmers and superior craftsmen. Although the French are justifiably proud of their history, they take particular care to impress upon their foreign contacts that their country is equally notable today for its technological achievements. Many of the advances in European high technology since the 1950s owe much to French technical know-how and political determination. This prowess is often more technological than commercial, however, because so many civil servants and state engineers in leadership positions lack business acumen. Hence success stories outside the military-industrial sphere such as Ariane and Airbus are matched by white elephants such as the Franco-British Concorde supersonic aircraft in the 1960s and the Superphenix ultrafast nuclear breeder since the 1980s. The recently commissioned nuclear-powered aircraft carrier *Charles de Gaulle*, whose cost is so great that it prevents France from having more than a single aircraft carrier for the foreseeable future, is a typical product of the engineers' (in this case the *ingénieurs de l'armement*) frequent preference for technical achievement over practicality.

Remarkable technical achievements are another reason why the defense and high-tech industry, as part and parcel of the advanced technological sector, is considered by a large portion of the French population as a great national asset. This attitude prevails among the most patriotic as well as other parts of society, including those who are more reticent in their support of the defense effort.[42] This widespread support gives French governments of whatever hue a reasonable measure of policy freedom and makes the defense and high-tech industrial sector largely immune to political changes.

Because this consensus was predicated upon the concept of national independence, and because there has been such a clean break in French history with World War II, the French defense industry has been built upon the idea that mounting a challenge to American dominance was an integral part of its mission. Only after 1945 did the United States become the obligatory reference point in the high-technology sector and thus not only a serious competitor, but one with a clear technological advantage as well as a political advantage in having the backing of the world's strongest power. It is not surprising, therefore, that armaments has remained the sector of French industry where the spirit of the *défi américain* (American challenge), to use the title of a very popular and influential French book written by the prominent journalist Jean-Jacques Servan-Schreiber in the 1960s, is most in evidence.

This posture was strengthened after the cold war by a perceived increase in American defense industrialists' aggressiveness on world markets—an attitude bred by the contraction of both home and foreign markets. It is manifest in two respects. First, U.S. industry has made a determined effort to eliminate competition from export markets, with the increasingly open help of the U.S. government.[43] Second, the defense industry has regrouped its forces and concentrated with greater speed and better effectiveness than its European and especially French counterparts, making the relationship between the two sides of the Atlantic even more unbalanced than before.

Since the 1960s, France has become an increasingly export-dependent arms maker.[44] After the end of the cold war, the dependency of its defense sector on its ability to sell abroad became an increasingly important element in defining French policy. In particular, it has become an important factor in DGA and defense industry decisions about the types of weapons to produce in France and, more specifically, their performance levels. In general terms, and certainly in the nonnuclear high-tech ventures, the number of weapons that can be absorbed by the French armed forces is too small to finance most large undertakings. This is why in recent years the capacity to export has always been an important parameter of French procurement decisions. It is also one of the motivations, much in evidence over the past decade, for the increased French preference for cooperative projects and joint ventures. Important programs such as the Hot and Roland missiles, the Tiger and NH-90 helicopters, and the Helios-1-A observation satellite have been undertaken in cooperation with European partners.[45]

Of the ongoing major French programs, more than half are in cooperation with Germany. Since the creation of the Eurocopter company, jointly owned by Aérospatiale (51 percent) and its German counterpart DASA

(49 percent), no new helicopter can be said to be purely French. A significant proportion of arms programs is also conducted in cooperation with the United Kingdom, as well as with Italy, Spain, and other partners. Matra, even before its merger with Aérospatiale and the subsequent merger in October 1999 of Matra-Aérospatiale with DASA of Germany and CASA of Spain, had created joint ventures with other European companies, intelligently placing itself at the center of advanced technological developments. The foremost missile producer in Europe, for instance, is Matra BAe Dynamics, a joint venture with British Aerospace. If Matra had been accepted as the main shareholder of Thomson-CSF, as was planned by the Juppé government in 1996, the resulting conglomerate would have drawn upon joint undertakings with BAe and DASA to become the sole sizable European missile manufacturer and one of the largest in the world, thus placing Matra at the center of a very important and rapidly growing sector.

Not only does such cooperation reduce basic costs, especially those for R&D, but it also leads to larger orders and output, thus contributing to a reduction in unit costs. This is especially true in the aerospace industry, which has an increasingly important civil side and is more internationalized than the sectors of land and naval armament. This logic holds at least as long as the competing national military requirements and the desire for national "just return" year by year and program by program (which could easily become the European equivalent of U.S. pork barrel) do not unduly inflate the expenditures. Exceptions exist: for instance, nuclear-capable equipment, including the technologically innovative but expensive and troubled aircraft carrier *Charles de Gaulle*, continues to be produced strictly nationally, although conversations about potential operational and industrial cooperation on nuclear-capable equipment are reported to have taken place with the British.

Politics has also played a role: the 1987 decision to pursue the development and production of the fighter aircraft Rafale, rather than participate in the European Fighter Aircraft (EFA) project with Germany, the United Kingdom, Italy, and Spain, was made under strong pressure from the well-organized and politically powerful Dassault group, then still headed by its founder, Marcel Dassault, and supported by the bulk of the armaments corps. That decision, however, was heavily criticized, and, given the great difficulty Dassault has had exporting the plane, after integrating the exports prospects into its production and pricing calculations, it is unlikely to be repeated.

In the more protected fields of land and naval armaments, some traditional French arms producers going back to the seventeenth-century *arsenaux*, today called the Groupement Industriel des Armements Terrestres (GIAT) for land equipment and the Direction des Constructions Navales (DCN) for naval procurement, are managed entirely by the state; many of the workers at the *arsenaux* enjoy civil service status as *ouvriers d'état*, a leftover from Napoleonic times with roots in the ancien régime. It follows that the need to make a profit in these state companies has not always matched that of their private sector competitors, who do not enjoy the privilege of a national bailout when things go badly wrong for them. Increasingly, though, the French state, acting both as shareholder and client, has demanded a more aggressive market-oriented attitude on their part, as evidenced by Defense Minister Richard's 1998 unprecedented decision to commission a frigate from a less expensive private sector shipyard instead of from the DCN.

As a result, exports prospects have become a key element in the initial decisions made on the viability of different programs. The Leclerc heavy battle tank, produced by state-owned GIAT, for instance, had been launched in the hope that it would sell in Europe and in the Middle East. GIAT was successful in selling this tank to the United Arab Emirates (UAE) in 1993; but this success ended in financial catastrophe after the down payment from the UAE was invested by the politically appointed leadership of the firm in U.S. dollar–denominated monetary futures at a tremendous loss. Such can be the consequences of political appointments and of poor financial and government controls. By contrast, the DCN, also owned by the state, has registered notable successes, such as a contract to equip Taiwan with frigates in 1992 and a similar, though smaller deal to equip Chile in 1999, without making subsequent calamitous management decisions.

Generally speaking, the quality of French military equipment is very high, and the fact that much of the French defense industry is still in state hands has not hindered its technological achievements or its ability to export abroad. But the financial management of the state-owned companies has too frequently been less than satisfactory, weighing inordinately on the hapless French taxpayer. And until the heavy losses incurred by those companies are redressed, there is no serious prospect of privatizing them.

So noted, the need to export has traditionally been one of the important parameters of French decisionmaking in military procurement. Private firms such as Matra Hautes Technologies and state-owned ones such as

Aérospatiale (now merged under Matra leadership) as well as Thomson-CSF (now Thalès), which was totally state owned until 1998 and is still partially state owned, have been remarkably successful exporters. French authorities are naturally keen to support the industry in obtaining foreign outlets for their products. France has become one of the largest arms exporters after the United States, according to congressional surveys about the international arms trade. The 1999 survey ranks France as second only to the United States both in 1998 and over the previous ten years.[46] Although some Americans have criticized France's supposedly "lax" export controls, it is fair to say that France has achieved these results by sticking faithfully to its commitments to international treaties and regimes, which is confirmed by the aforementioned congressional surveys.

After the end of the cold war and the subsequent shrinking of the world armaments market, however, world competition became fiercer, and the international position of the French arms exporters grew increasingly fragile. This was largely due to a new aggressiveness on the part of their American competitors, who were equally concerned about their capacity to survive in a smaller international market, and for whom export markets had gone from being a useful complement to the domestic U.S. purchases to becoming an essential and sometimes vital component in their calculations of profitability. Because exports were so important for the industry, public authorities in both the legislative and the executive branches were pressed into stronger action to secure foreign markets from the competition. Congress took greater interest in the issue, and the executive, even at the highest level, was involved in inducing foreign governments to buy U.S. military equipment. Even more important for relations with France, the U.S. government, especially after the election of President Clinton, with his vaunted concentration on domestic and economic affairs, wanted to be seen as taking an active role in promoting job-creating exports. This new focus created great concern among French defense industrial circles that the United States was bent on pushing French and European defense industrialists into a second-tier position, where their contribution would be no more than that of subcontractors, specialized in market segments but incapable of launching full major programs.

In the French view, the American attitude in the Gulf region after the successful reconquest of Kuwait by the U.S.-led international coalition corroborated that alarming theory. After 1945, the United States had followed in the footsteps of the declining British Empire as the main protector of the Arab monarchies and had naturally obtained many defense contracts as a result. But its close relations with Israel had induced mixed feelings toward it among the Gulf states. That created openings for other powers, foremost among which was France, whose position on the Israeli-Arab conflict the Arabs believed to be more balanced than that of the United States. Also, U.S. legislation limited the ability of American industry to compete on equal terms, since Israel's supporters in Congress had mandated strict restrictions on sales of advanced military products to declared opponents of Israel such as Saudi Arabia (though it was a close U.S. ally) and Qatar. France had therefore obtained major contracts, in particular in the United Arab Emirates and to a lesser extent in Saudi Arabia. The French defense industry had slowly built a dominant position in Qatar, a nation that was always ready to keep a respectful distance from the United States.[47] As already indicated, these contracts were of major, and in some cases paramount, importance to the survival of the French defense industry as an independent and relatively self-sufficient entity on a world scale.

After the Gulf War, American industrialists saw their chance to compensate for some of the reduction in U.S. and Western defense equipment orders by inducing Gulf states to rely on defense products from the country that had contributed the most to preventing domination of the region by Iraq. Furthermore, this commercial offensive enjoyed the active, though quiet, support of the George H. W. Bush administration, thus broadening institutional support for such sales, which was usually confined to the Pentagon. During the Clinton presidency, which energetically and ostentatiously supported U.S. arms exports, the psychological effect in France of such high-level political activism was compounded by the public nature of Washington's salesmanship. Because the administration was trumpeting its concentration on domestic objectives, it justified its international commitments in economic terms. Telephone calls from the president and Cabinet members to Gulf leaders in which the Americans pressed for the purchase of a particular U.S.-made product rather than foreign ones were leaked to and reported in the press. The French government adopted a similar tactic, especially after the election of President Chirac.

To French defense industrialists and their counterparts in the civil service, naturally inclined to be defensive in response to American competition, the newly aggressive behavior of the United States was chilling. Coming at a time when both domestic and foreign markets for the French defense industry were contracting, it fed fears that the United States wanted to eliminate the European, and especially the French, defense industry as a self-standing entity. In such views, the aim of the Americans was to tolerate the continued existence of European capabilities in this sector only as long as they became dependent on U.S. firms, either as subcontractors or as suppliers of limited and specialized equipment. Throughout most of the 1990s, this opinion prevailed in the French armaments establishment. Distrust of the U.S. defense industry grew, even while the relationship between the men responsible for the armaments sector was generally respectful and sometimes excellent. The 1996 decision by France to end its participation in the MEADS (Medium-range Extended Air Defense System) ballistic defense program with the United States, Germany, and Italy was based on real budgetary constraints as well as on skepticism about the seriousness of the U.S. commitment to the final development of that program. It would be wrong to deny, however, that some suspicion of the United States had permeated French thinking in defense circles, even as the French-American relationship was otherwise improving. In this respect, the abandonment of MEADS by the French government can fairly be interpreted as a result of a growing concern on the part of the French defense industrial establishment about the increasing might of the United States. In the private sector, however, the prospect of a transatlantic marketplace is considered sufficiently attractive for a firm like Thalès to have embarked on an ambitious series of agreements with the much larger U.S. firm Raytheon.

Restructuring has become an important issue for all defense industries in the United States as well as in Europe. In France, however, the difficulty of this process was compounded by the equally important need to privatize the large portion of the sector that had been in state hands for a long time. Although the two issues—restructuring and privatization—remain conceptually separate, it is difficult to describe the two processes separately because they were tightly intertwined in France in recent years. This apprehensive mood was compounded by the fact that the American weapons makers, already enjoying a competitive advantage because of the size of their domestic market and the larger share of the gross national product spent by the United States on their defense effort, regrouped their forces and reorganized to meet the challenges of the post–cold war era with a speed unmatched by their European counterparts. This movement, made possible by the greater flexibility and ruthlessness built into the U.S. economic and social environment, was encouraged by the Pentagon. William Perry, the U.S. secretary of defense, is said to have taken a personal part in 1993 in telling the CEOs of the largest American defense contractors that industrial overcapacity could only be brought to an end by reducing the number of corporate entities in the sector. The meeting during which this view was conveyed has been widely labeled in the press as the "Long Knives Dinner" or the "Last Supper." Even if the federal authorities cannot be accused of directly participating in the industrial arrangements that followed and led to the mega-mergers of 1995–97, it is plain that the restructuring originated at the Pentagon.[48] It is in no way surprising that the single client of the defense industry would play an important role in defining the optimum market and supply conditions in such an important sector. But the massive reorganization of the American defense industry has not taken place in a political vacuum, with market forces as its sole determining factor. On the contrary, Pentagon involvement was both powerful and visible.

This did not go unnoticed in Paris, where the restructuring of the French defense industry was being constantly delayed, with consequences not only for France but for the European defense industry as a whole.[49] It can fairly be said that "the main obstacle to the restructuring of the European defense industry has been the slow pace at which the French weapons industry has adapted."[50]

Between 1990 and 1995, the heavy cost of restructuring such a major industry, particularly the reductions in employment, frightened successive French governments, especially because parliamentary and presidential elections were due in 1993 and 1995, respectively. Furthermore, President Mitterrand was personally reluctant to diminish defense spending. As a result, reductions in defense expenditure were made surreptitiously rather than openly. Defense budgets voted at the beginning of each year were based on the assumption that defense spending would not be diminished, or would even grow, but the appropriation bills voted at the end of the year showed that much of the spending had in fact been reallocated to other departments or canceled altogether through widespread recourse to the *arbitrage budgétaire* procedure, whereby the Finance Ministry's concerns for financial orthodoxy eventually prevailed over considerations for the predictability of the armed forces' budget and equipment. Consequently, "a certain form of budgetary arbitrariness reigned."[51]

Upon President Chirac's election in 1995, necessary decisions on industrial restructuring were made in coordination with the major re-adaptation of the French military apparatus that the president had announced during the election campaign.[52] The centerpiece of the government's effort was to have been the privatization of Thomson, whereby its defense arm, Thomson-CSF, was to be sold and entrusted to the Matra company, part of the Lagardère group, and separated from its civil electronics wing, loss-making Thomson Multimedia (TMM). The last was effectively to be given away to the Korean group Daewoo for a single franc to reduce the ongoing cost to the taxpayer. When a loud political and public outcry ensued, the independent committee in charge of overseeing privatizations voided the decision on the grounds that the TMM project was contrary to the public interest in that it was detrimental to the interests of the Treasury. This decision undid the entire privatization of the Thomson group and delayed the restructuring of the French defense industry, with repercussions for Europe as a whole.

French restructuring would in fact have to wait until after the June 1997 legislative election, which was called early by President Chirac and resulted in the defeat of his political allies. In the event, the new Socialist government decided to privatize only Thomson-CSF (leaving TMM in state hands) and adjudicating it to the rival bidder to Matra, the Alcatel group.[53] Because the latter was far less involved in a web of European alliances than the former, the decision was widely described as inspired by national rather than European considerations.[54] Still, Thalès (formerly Thomson-CSF) has done very well since, and with the decision by Alcatel to divest itself of its noncore assets in 2000–01, it has become an autonomous firm, able to pursue an independent policy of foreign alliances, including some seventeen joint projects with Raytheon of the United States. Among them, the most significant is the agreement announced in 2000 between the two companies to set up a major joint venture in air defense electronics systems.[55] It was thus more difficult to reorganize the European-wide defense electronics sector in a rational way than if Matra had been chosen.[56] By ending a long period of uncertainty, however, this decision made the restructuring of the European defense sector possible.[57] Subsequently, DASA and British Aerospace started planning a merger,[58] which foundered in 1998 on BAe's decision to purchase the defense electronics interests of British GEC, the first European mega-merger in the defense sector.[59] This in turn led DaimlerChrysler, the main shareholder of DASA, to take a controlling interest in Spanish CASA in April 1999 and then to turn back to Matra-Aérospatiale, with which it announced a merger in October 1999 to establish a company named EADS.[60] The process of European restructuring, largely in response to the earlier moves in the United States, though with a seven-year delay, had completed at least its initial phase.[61] In the meantime, French and to some extent European defense industrialists and their public sector counterparts sensed that their U.S. opposite numbers were simply too strong to embark on transatlantic cooperative ventures, much less mergers. Furthermore, uncertainty about the future structure of the European industry made it difficult for any major cooperative decisions to be taken, either by American or by

European firms.[62] The gap between the reorganized U.S. side and the unfinished state of European restructuring was simply too wide, at least until late 1999, for genuine transatlantic enterprises to take place. It is to be noted that, largely under French leadership, the governments of France, Germany, Italy, and the United Kingdom, countries that represent some 85 percent of the European defense industrial capacity, had decided on November 12, 1996, to create a common structure to manage armaments production and procurement, the Joint Armaments Cooperation Organization, generally known by its French initials OCCAR.[63] Thus the scene was set for the first time for the implementation of a common armaments policy. This structure was further refined in agreements on September 9, 1998, in Farnborough,[64] making it possible for OCCAR eventually to become the armaments agency of the European Union.[65] That prospect would open once the merger of the WEU into the EU, decided at the European summit of Cologne in June 1999, had been achieved. Furthermore, the Amsterdam Treaty of 1997 stated that a European armaments policy was a goal to be achieved in the framework of the European Security and Defense Policy (ESDP); as an intergovernmental process it would be more likely than the integrationist approach to convince national authorities to relinquish some of their control over such an important dimension of sovereignty. The rapid progress of the Saint-Malo process led the four governments of OCCAR, plus Sweden, Spain, and the Netherlands, to sign a letter of intent indicating their support for OCCAR within the European Union, probably through a special treaty among themselves. Such an agreement would eliminate the principle of "just return," which makes international cooperation in armaments production particularly costly, and would set up an armaments agency capable of procuring, ordering, and purchasing directly the armaments produced by two or more participating countries while not excluding the national programs of any participant. This should in the medium term contribute to streamlining the European defense industry by eliminating duplication.

At this writing in late 2001, the long transatlantic waiting game may be coming to an end. Not only are French and European worries over American structural superiority less acute after a period of genuine European restructuring, but many in the United States are beginning to wonder aloud whether the European allies should have wider access to the American market, either through transatlantic mergers or direct sales.[66] The eloquent speech given by Deputy Secretary of Defense John Hamre on the "globalization" of the industry on May 5, 1999, and the remarks attributed to Under

Secretary for Procurement Jacques Gansler in July of the same year, according to which transatlantic mergers were now a possibility, provided a sign of the growing desire of U.S. Defense Department officials to avoid being faced with nonchoices when the next generation of weapons has to be purchased.[67] There are serious limitations on the U.S. side, however, because technology sharing with allies is often made impossible by Pentagon worries about high-technology falling into the wrong hands and the uncertainty in the Bush administration over which road to take in these matters. This explains the late 1999 statements by the CEOs of DASA and BAe Systems, according to which the best way for their companies to take on a transatlantic dimension would be by purchasing U.S. companies rather than through merging with them.[68] One result of the U.S. restructuring, largely implemented along functional lines, has been that a single U.S. company makes a number of key products. This could create supplier monopolies, an unsatisfactory situation for both the cost and the quality of weapons. A window of opportunity has therefore been opened, signaled by the November 1998 memorandum among the United States, France, Germany, and Great Britain, rationalizing and to some extent harmonizing national regulations in twelve principles of "good conduct."[69]

Many elements need to be refined, however, to make feasible the aim of creating a transatlantic marketplace in armaments.[70] The American side is rightly concerned about quality, especially in terms of precision and accuracy. Some concerns also have been voiced about secrecy[71] and the danger of untrustworthy states gaining access to high-technology weapons. However, these worries are to a large extent exaggerated, fed by industrial rivalries, because nothing in the French attitude toward so-called rogue states justifies such fears. French export procedures are particularly strict and have fully integrated new and comprehensive regimes such as the Missile Technology Control Regime (MTCR), to a degree comparable to and in some cases stricter than those of its main Western partners. On the European and especially French side, other concerns exist. It is especially important to these countries that security of supply of arms or parts be ensured, including against possible future congressionally mandated restrictions—assurances that are hard to obtain in the U.S. system. For all partners, the consequences of mergers for local employment are most important,[72] and some guarantees will be expected, especially if some industrial alliances are lopsided—that is, dominated by a single nation. Finally, from a French viewpoint, it is essential, before embarking upon transatlantic mergers or close cooperative ventures with U.S. partners, that the playing field be leveled: European access to U.S. procurement must be comparable to that enjoyed by the United States in European markets, and no one European country should be given privileged access. In this respect, it is counterproductive to maintain politically motivated discrimination against France, as exemplified in the informal categories that are said to be used in some documents of the Defense Department at congressional urging. European restructuring will in any case make such discrimination increasingly untenable if Europe as a whole is not to be excluded from the U.S. market. Americans have complained loudly and consistently about the unlikely prospect of a "Fortress Europe" in the armaments field.[73] A transatlantic marketplace will demand a reasonable and balanced opening of U.S. procurement to European, including French, tenderers.

CHAPTER FIVE

A Rekindled Alliance

FRANCE AND THE United States have been a quarrelsome pair, yet their mutual interests force them to work out the terms of a revived and thriving alliance. Separation is precluded because they are partners in multiple collective and bilateral endeavors. There can be no conclusive resolution of their differences, since that would mean at least one of them, probably France, relinquishing important aspects of its distinctive national identity and political personality. Consequently, they must learn to live with the accumulated baggage from their troubled past: injured pride, feelings of ingratitude, real or imagined offenses—all the negatives intertwined with the positive experience as comrades in arms in the great tests of the twentieth century.

Complete harmony on outlook and policy is not, therefore, the appropriate goal of efforts to improve French-American ties. An element of tension and rivalry will linger even as the two countries pursue joint enterprises. Jacques Chirac's bon mot on the troubled partnership between Paris and Washington, is apt; he remarked: "[Relations] have been, are, and will always be conflictive and excellent. . . . The U.S. finds France unbearably pretentious. And we find the U.S. unbearably hegemonic."[1] It would be fruitless to expend energy on trying to instill a common French-American vision of the world. Neither country lacks a conception of how the world should be organized and managed. Rather each country has a tendency to fashion a vision that would see its national conceptions of the international order dominate. This would confirm the virtue of cooperating on the many tasks that lie before them.

The American Perspective

The United States' official attitude toward the French "anomaly" has varied. At different times, France has been treated as a dangerous heretic within the Western camp, as a nuisance that was vexing but could be ignored for the most part, and at other times it has been considered as a valuable partner to be enlisted in common causes at a reasonable price. This lack of consistency is unsurprising. The United States' adjustment to the cold war's end has been incremental. There has been no grand design built on a clear, comprehensive view of American interests and a crisp delineation of which responsibilities should be shared with allies, on what basis. Bold and divisive initiatives, such as NATO enlargement, have been interspersed with periods of drift. The reaction to episodic crises has played a larger role in shaping the American frame of reference than have deliberate exercises in strategic blueprinting. Accordingly, Washington's attitude toward France is derived from the wider desultory debate over the terms of the Euro-American partnership. It has been largely driven by the exigencies of crisis management—in the Gulf, Bosnia, Kosovo, Afghanistan. Although there are discernible recurrent themes, the harmonics have shifted according to circumstance.

France has not been prominent enough in the United States' field of strategic vision to require concentrated attention and a deliberate policy. Rather, France has been only one piece of the larger strategic puzzle— whether that be revalidating and renovating NATO, devising a pancontinental security system that encompasses Russia, dealing with ethnic violence in the Balkans, containing the latent Iraqi threat in the Gulf, or building a rule-based global trade regime. An important and often awkward player, France has not achieved the distinction of being singled out for a customized policy. Yet to recount the rocky course of French-American relations is to make the case for a deliberate effort to fashion a bilateral relationship clear in purpose and consistent in method.

The dividends would be worth the investment. As the West's multilateral institutions move into a new phase, with the inescapable transformation in the terms of engagement between the United States and Europe, it is all the more important for Washington to focus on France. After all, by dint of will and location France will continue to play a key role in an EU readying itself by degrees to be an independent force on the world scene. Defining a "French" policy is integral to the larger process of devising both a transatlantic strategy that accords with new realities—and a wider global design.

The French construct of a multipolar world diverges significantly from the American worldview, even if the two approaches are not diametrically opposed. In its goal of curbing the American "hyperpower," in its ambition to create within the EU an independent center for security decisionmaking as well as for organizing possible military operations, in its dedication to amending the international monetary regime and to strengthening the trade regime so as to delimit U.S. influence, France challenges American conceptions and American power. But does the discordant note habitually struck by Paris pose such a threat to American interests as to call for a campaign to counter French initiatives with a vigorous diplomatic counteroffensive? Probably not—for two reasons. First, the United States' predominance in almost all spheres is so secure that its influence is only marginally affected by French efforts to cut Uncle Sam down to size. Second, because France increasingly strives to magnify its power by acting through the European Union, there are no obvious places to draw lines in the sand between Washington and Paris that would not intersect the broader U.S.-EU relationship. On those French-inspired EU actions that irk the United States (especially in the security area), it is hard to separate welcome European capability building from unwelcome intrusion into areas that Washington prefers to keep to itself.

Although the net effect of France's strategy of embedding its interests within a common European position is to strengthen its hand while creating disincentives for the United States to attack Paris-inspired initiatives, a strategy of isolating France on a particular issue can still be effective. The American campaign against the European Security and Defense Policy establishing a significant military planning structure independent of NATO is a case in point. But Washington can only go so far in trying to drive wedges between France and its more Atlanticist partners, lest it jeopardize the larger project of EU construction that serves long-term U.S. interests. There is no gainsaying the influence that Paris exerts within the EU. Its pairing with Germany as the twin motors of the integration process, whatever strains the partnership may be showing, puts France in a pivotal position. A skillful and persistent diplomacy exploits it to the hilt. During a period when the pattern of Euro-American relations is being reconfigured by the implementation of the European Monetary Union (EMU) and the first serious moves toward creation of an EU defense policy, American decisionmakers will be hard pressed to synchronize European policy at multiple levels (the EU and national) and across issues that are linked by intra-union politics. In order to do so successfully, they must pay close attention to

France—and to the need, whenever reasonably possible, to reconcile U.S. and French perspectives.

A businesslike approach to dealings with France that avoids rhetorical exchanges and overreaction to perceived provocation is both desirable and feasible. Mindful that France does not have the weight to shape the thinking of other major governments or the means to prevent the United States from achieving its most important objectives, Washington should work with Paris where practical, forbear where necessary. The essence of such a strategy was sketched by George Kennan who, in coupling France with China, characterized them as "both proud people. . . . Both are conscious of being the bearers of a great cultural tradition. They like to be left alone. . . . Our policy should be to treat them with the most exquisite courtesy and respect on the official level, but not expect too much from them. . . . They are not going to love us no matter what we do."[2] This unsentimental approach has the virtue of excising the emotional factor from what so often has been a fraught relationship. Thus U.S. policymakers would be unfazed by France's supposed lack of appreciation for either American good intentions or past sacrifices made on its behalf. At the same time, the unsentimental approach would deny French leaders the status enhancement they get from verbal and diplomatic jousts with the American colossus.

However, an arm's-length diplomacy with a close ally, even one as prickly as France, has its drawbacks. It weakens the presumption of shared interests, which is the only sound basis for solidifying alliance bonds. Matter-of-fact cooperation on individual issues needs to be bolstered by more active engagement. That will not prove easy, as the foregoing account makes clear. Although the two governments have found pragmatic grounds for cooperation on a number of important matters, they do not fit comfortably together as a team. Unlike the long-standing habits of concert between Washington and London, or the strategic partnership with Berlin, the Franco-American pair must labor to find satisfactory grounds for working together issue by issue, episode by episode. Efforts to end reflexive mutual criticism, to mute the rhetoric of rivalry, and to avoid falling prey to stereotypical mutual images should manage to remove some of the obstacles to a more productive relationship. But that modest accomplishment is not sufficient to instill instincts of partnership. Engagement for the United States means accepting that the French worldview is deeply held and is not liable to be brought fully into line with Washington's, no matter how earnest the efforts to do so. Consequently, agreement and concert can occur only when there is at least minimal accommodation of French perspectives and

French concerns. That was the tack taken by Washington during the Kosovo crisis, with productive results. By contrast, the failure to reach agreement on the terms of France's reentry into NATO indicated how ticklish an attempted exercise in mutual accommodation can be, especially when the very structure of the relationship is at issue. When that approach is unavailing, the wise policy is to seal it off from other, more productive areas of Franco-American dealings.

Only by concentrating on shared objectives can the two countries reap the rewards of cooperation. Working out the modalities of collaboration on a case-by-case basis amounts to something less than full partnership, but a routinized partnership among parties of uneven strength inescapably subordinates the weaker to the stronger. The status of junior partner is intolerable for France, whatever concessions Washington might make to its singular pride and exalted self-image. The United States' sense of superiority is so strong, its drive to lead, direct, and instruct too ingrained to adjust to accommodating a partner whose sensitivities are as acute as France's. The more modest objective of adhering to forms of address modulated to French sensibilities is probably at the limits of American adaptability. There also are occasions when the United States could gracefully concede to France a share of the limelight and the glory when a common enterprise succeeds, as in Bosnia in 1995 and then in Kosovo. As Philip Gordon has observed, "In Paris a little bit of *gloire* goes a long way."[3]

The French Perspective

France has quite a different set of choices. For obvious structural reasons, they are more limited than those of the United States. In practical terms, the choices before France are different versions of Europeanism. One version borders on the nationalistic. Because the European project was largely the brainchild of Frenchmen, a deeply felt sense of French history and destiny has permeated the country's vision of Europe. At the official level and in the country as a whole, many view Europe as a "France writ large," not only in terms of its political organization, but also in its dealings with other countries. There exists a prevalent conception of Europe as an international actor that is not only autonomous but also revisionist in its rejection of U.S. leadership. At the same time, most "Europeanists" believe there is in the European project an underlying sense of belonging to a common Western community that includes the United States. Moreover, a more autonomous

Europe, according to this widespread French conception, could encourage this sense of Euro-American commonality, because it would diminish the fears of overdependency on America. In addition, there is the realization that the shape of Europe will depend not only on French views and preferences but also on those of its partners. For most of the fourteen other members of the EU, the European project cannot be implemented in opposition to Washington. On the contrary, its success and its acceptability will depend on its remaining compatible with the wider Western frameworks. Both in the political-military and in the political-economic dimensions of the West, this is demonstrably the case. The difficulty lies in the manner by which the allies on the two sides of the Atlantic approach the union-building project.

A stronger, more cohesive Europe is a potential source of valued international support for American policy, even if this naturally implies that the United States will have to take European views more fully into account than it does now. The melding of viewpoints into a common policy will be inhibited, though, if each approaches the other already locked into inflexible positions. On the European side, that may be due to the laborious and fragile process of building a policy consensus. On the American side, it may be due to strained relations between the executive and a Congress that vies to exercise its own influence on the country's external relations. The risk is greatest on trade issues, where the pattern is readily discernible. The challenge is to exploit the construction of a unified Europe that will strengthen transatlantic relations and not become a source of division. It behooves the United States to accept that modification of the Western system, which it has largely defined and that has served it so well, is unavoidable. It behooves France to realize that to play the European card relentlessly so as to bolster its standing on issues of contention with the United States will deepen American distrust of French intentions and thereby slow down the process of European construction. Both countries will be losers unless Washington and Paris find ways of working in tandem on the transition to a balanced partnership.

The Existential Question for France

By making "Europe" the leitmotiv of its international posture, France has created for itself problems of an existential nature. The French project for Europe is inherently ambiguous. It is conceived as an instrument to increase French significance in the world while its power diminishes in relative terms. Simultaneously, it is a way to collectively empower European nations whose individual historical experiences, attitudes toward international conflict, and notions of the role of the state in society vary considerably. This ambiguity makes adherence to a genuinely "federalist" agenda for the European Union highly implausible, for to abolish France's place as a sovereign state on the world scene is to negate one of the two goals of French policy, that of magnifying French presence and influence. Progress in realizing the objectives of the Saint-Malo process, in entrenching EMU, and in enlargement make it impossible to beg the question of the compatibility of the two French ambitions contained in its European project. Initiatives taken by other European countries, above all Germany, are forcing the issue. In May 2000, Germany's foreign minister, Joschka Fischer, unveiled an openly federalist vision of Europe in a landmark speech to the European parliament.[4] It placed the French establishment in exactly the type of quandary that it had been trying to avoid through creative equivocation and constructive ambiguity. Jacques Chirac, addressing the Bundestag in June 2000, grasped the nettle in offering his model of the union's future. He proposed the creation of a treaty-based "pioneer group" of like-minded countries, ready to merge their policies more completely than the rest of their union partners, the Common Foreign and Security Policy (CFSP) prominent among them.[5] Still, Chirac sidestepped the sensitive issues: foremost among them the consolidation of national diplomatic establishments, and the Europeanization of national capabilities, including France's nuclear forces and permanent seat on the UN Security Council.

The speeches by Chirac and Fischer were the opening statements in an intensifying communitywide debate over the EU's future constitutional structure. The union's impending enlargement is forcing a reappraisal of its hybrid structure and complicated decisionmaking processes. Present arrangements have served France well. Now it is searching for a viable alternative to the German federalist model, one that conserves the essence of France's national autonomy while strengthening the EU institutions in ways that advance French interests and ideas.

Indeterminacy as to what Europe will look like, how it will make policy, and how it will conduct diplomacy leaves the United States uneasy. It has no fixed reference marks for restructuring Euro-American relations.[6] It is asked to support a process whose destination no one knows. Neither France nor the United States can predict where this road will finally lead. The United States is tolerant of the complexities of the ongoing projects. In the short term, this fluidity may be welcome to a Washington that values its freedom of action and flexibility in dealing with its European partners. Perpetual irresolution of what Europe is and is able to do, however, handicaps both sides in their pursuit of common interests. Much remains to be done to build institutions in the political field that will earn them the respect of their counterparts in the domain of trade. Rotating presidencies every six months; a cumbersome, multilayered voting system; powers divided between the Council of Ministers and the EU Commission—all these elements inspire little confidence in the EU's American interlocutors. A CFSP that cannot give Washington a reliable partner fails all concerned. France, as the critical party to the European debate, serves the interest of the United States as well as its own by advancing the process of defining an EU that is an open, constructive partner.

U.S.-French Bilateralism

The potentially profound effect of the European project on the structure and workings of the Euro-American relationship means that Franco-American bilateralism in the here and now cannot succeed without a strong multilateral process. France's choice in making the EU the centerpiece of its foreign policy places a premium on shaping new modes of EU-U.S. consultation and coordination. The absence of a permanent transatlantic institution dealing with nonsecurity issues is a particular liability for France, because it enjoys neither the closeness of its partners' network of U.S. contacts nor a sense of full membership in the NATO structures that facilitate dialogue beyond military matters, narrowly defined. This is not to say that the French official position advocates the creation of such an institution—quite the contrary. The situational logic does suggest that French-American relations would be a main beneficiary of this development. This could take the form of a strengthened U.S.-EU structure that goes beyond the Action Plan of 1995 inaugurated under the rubric of the New Transatlantic Agenda. Today, in addition to the diplomatic representations in Washington and Brussels, biannual summit meetings take place between the U.S. president and the president of the European Commission; these are supplemented by ministerial-level meetings. But they are not sufficient. The summit itself is somewhat contrived, because the president of the commission is not the leader of the union in the sense that he operates under the strict supervision of the member states. Moreover, a considerable portion of policy is beyond his purview, especially the increasingly important security dimension. An

EU-U.S. dialogue in which the European partner has limited authority to speak for Europe is bound to be disappointing, especially when the other party acts under increasingly close congressional scrutiny.[7]

Among the present relationships between major nations in the Western world, the French-American one stands alone in not being buttressed by a strong permanent bilateral process—one that allows decisionmakers to meet and inform one another of emerging policies before they are set in concrete. In its absence, the relationship is subject to disturbance by unanticipated initiatives. Intimate understanding is needed of the political processes and attitudes that explain both the positions taken by the other country and why they are presented in a particular manner. The tone chosen by leaders and the domestic and regional circumstances in which initiatives are taken are often as important as the decision itself. They can only be understood abroad when there is knowledge of the political environment within which decisions are reached, as well as the limitations under which political leaders operate.

These circumstances plead for France to pay much more attention to the complexities of the U.S. political process than it has until now. Because France is a unitary state, where on every policy decision the final word is given at the highest echelons of the governmental structure—sometimes affecting even minute details—French officials frequently assume that other systems operate the same way. French diplomats have traditionally been happy to believe that a decision had been reached in Washington when the State Department had given it its blessing, only to feel frustrated when that decision was rescinded under the influence of another department, the Congress, or special interests outside the government. Few Frenchmen can boast of understanding the complexities of decisionmaking in a federal system marked by the separation of powers among branches of government, though they have learned much in recent years. The French need to make a considerable effort in this direction.

There is need for a reciprocal effort on the American side. Too often, Washington's instinctive response to French declarations and diplomatic initiatives is either dismissal or suspicion that a sinister ulterior motive inspires them, even when they appear to tally with U.S. postures. A better understanding of France in the United States is unlikely in itself to create the kind of osmosis that exists between the political and intellectual establishments of Britain and Germany on one hand and of the United States on the other. French positions will remain distinctive, and France will remain somewhat of a tribunitarian presence within the Western camp, and especially within NATO. Paris will continue to warn against the dangers of undue dependence on Washington in a more forceful manner than other major allies do. Still, it is possible to voice such concerns and to make them more comprehensible to Americans.

The Euro-American debate on the terms of their mutual engagement is just beginning. As it unfolds, France is destined to be an influential protagonist. It would be costly for all if that debate were distorted by the ritual duels between Washington and Paris. The delicate processes of refining modes of cooperation between NATO and the EU, and between the United States and Europe, can too easily be diverted into blind alleys.

All empires disappear, and so do imperiums. The only question is how long it takes for them to do so. How long will the American hegemony prevail? The historical trend is toward the benign multipolar international system whose modus operandi is multilateralism, which France desires and the United States finds uncomfortable. France's impulse to force the pace reinforces the United States' disinclination to yield gracefully to the dictates of time and circumstance. Those instincts, if unbridled, are the worst enemies of both countries' plans—and a threat to cooperation among the Western democracies. Conversely, closer mutual attention can bear fruit, precisely because positions are held so strongly. A vigorous and frank dialogue holds out the best hope of making compatible American and French visions of the twenty-first century.

Notes

Chapter One

1. On the history of the French-American relationship, see Charles G. Cogan, *Oldest Allies, Guarded Friends: The United States and France since 1940* (Westport, Conn.: Praeger, 1994).

2. See Richard N. Haass and Robert E. Litan, "Globalization and Its Discontents: Navigating the Dangers of a Tangled World," *Foreign Affairs*, vol. 77 (May–June 1998), pp. 2–6; Mortimer B. Zuckerman, "A Second American Century," *Foreign Affairs*, vol. 77 (May–June 1998), pp. 18–31; Simon Serfaty, "Memories of Leadership," *Brown Journal of World Affairs*, vol. 5 (Summer–Fall 1998), p. 12.

3. See Robert Anderson and Arthur A. Hartman, "France and the United States: Charting a New Course," Policy Paper Washington: Atlantic Council of the United States (February 1995).

4. See Jacques Andréani, "Monde unipolaire, ou les tentations de la puissance," *Défense* (December 1997), pp. 42–46; Hubert Védrine, "Il est de l'ordre de la critique légitime de mettre en cause l'unilatéralisme américain," *Le Monde*, March 16, 1999.

5. See John O'Sullivan, "How the West Was Spun," *National Interest* (Spring 1999), pp. 87–96.

6. See Serfaty, "Memories of Leadership," p. 10: "With many of the allies suspicious of U.S. intent and the ability to explain what it does and execute what it says, there is limited will for followership because there is little understanding of the proposed leadership."

7. Guillaume Guindey, *The International Monetary Tangle: Myths and Realities* (Oxford: Basil Blackwell, 1977), pp. 85–88.

8. Marie-France Garaud and Didier Motchane, "Du consentement à l'assujettissement," *Le Monde*, June 11, 1999. On the limits of anti-Americanism in France today, see "En France, l'antiaméricanisme structuré apparaît minoritaire et politique," *Le Monde*, January 6–7, 2002.

Chapter Two

1. Richard Haass, "What to Do with American Primacy," *Foreign Affairs*, vol. 78 (September–October 1999), pp. 37–49; Charles Kupchan, "After Pax Americana, Benign Power, Regional Integration, and the Sources of a Stable Multipolarity," *International Security*, vol. 23 (Fall 1998), pp. 40–79.

2. James Baker, Speech to Berlin Press Club, December 3, 1989, USIA press release, December 4, 1989.

3. Simon Serfaty, "France–Etats-Unis: La querelle permanente," *Relations Internationales et Stratégiques*, no. 25 (Spring 1997), pp. 52–59.

4. Dominique Moïsi, "The Trouble with France," *Foreign Affairs* (May–June 1998), p. 97.

5. See, for instance, middle-school textbooks such as *Histoire géographie 4ème* (Paris: Hatier, 1998), pp. 56, 58; and *Histoire géographie 4ème* (Paris: Belin, 1998), p. 42; and texts used in the university such as Olivier Chaline, *La France au 18ème siècle* (Paris: Belin, 1996), pp. 38, 265, 272, 273.

6. In the French parliament on January 14, 1998, for example, Prime Minister Lionel Jospin accused his right-of-center opponents of being the heirs to the supporters of slavery and to the *anti-dreyfusard* movement.

7. Moïsi, "The Trouble with France," p. 96.

8. Daniel Jouve, Alice Jouve, and Alvin Grossman, *Paris, Birthplace of the U.S.A.* (Paris: Gründ, 1997). The American film *Jefferson in Paris* was a hit in France. One of the most prestigious schools in Paris, St. Louis de Gonzague, where much of the French establishment is educated, is known as "Franklin," the name of the street where it is situated.

9. Jean-Baptiste Duroselle, *L'abîme, 1939–1945* (Paris: Imprimerie Nationale, 1982), pp. 491–95.

10. Pierre Melandri, "The Troubled Friendship: France and the United States, 1945–1989," in Geir Lundestad, ed., *No End to Alliance: The United States and Western Europe: Past, Present, and Future* (St. Martin's, 1998), pp. 112–13.

11. Charles de Gaulle, Washington, April 25, 1960: "Si matériellement parlant, la balance peut sembler égale entre les deux camps qui divisent l'univers, moralement elle ne l'est pas. La France pour sa part a choisi; elle a choisi d'être du côté des peuples libres, elle a choisi d'être avec vous." (If in material terms the balance between the two camps that divide the world may seem even, it is not so on moral grounds. For her own part, France has made a choice; she has chosen the side of the free peoples, she has chosen to be with you.) Charles de Gaulle, *Discours et Messages*, Vol. 3: *Avec le renouveau Mai 1958–Juillet 1962* (Paris: Plon, 1970), p. 198. Unless otherwise indicated, all translations of French passages that appear in this book are by the authors.

12. See Hubert Védrine, *Les mondes de François Mitterrand, 1981–1995* (Paris: Fayard, 1996).

13. Philip H. Gordon, *A Certain Idea of France: French Security Policy and the Gaullist Legacy* (Princeton University Press, 1993), part 3; Guillaume Parmentier, *Le*

retour de l'histoire (Brussels: Editions Complexe, 1993); and Pierre Lellouche, "France in Search of Security," *Foreign Affairs*, vol. 72 (Spring 1993), pp. 122–31.

14. An authoritative examination of Gaullist strategy and the intra-alliance debate that it engendered is provided by Frédéric Bozo, *Two Strategies for Europe* (Lanham, Md.: Rowman and Littlefield, 2000).

15. Gordon, *A Certain Idea of France*, p. 185.

16. Michel Tatu, "France, Etats-Unis: Pour le meilleur et pour le pire," *Politique Internationale* (Spring 1995), pp. 321–32.

17. François Mitterrand, "Voeux au peuple Français," December 31, 1989, quoted in Frédéric Bozo and Jérôme Paolini, "L'Allemagne, l'Europe et la France," *Politique Etrangère* (January 1990), p. 119.

18. Ibid., p. 751.

19. Speech at the Forum de l'Ecole Supérieure de Guerre, in Ministère de la défense, *Propos sur la défense*, no. 20 (March–April 1991).

20. The French-German relationship is insightfully analyzed in Philip H. Gordon, *France, Germany and the Western Alliance* (Boulder, Colo.: Westview, 1995); and in David Calleo and B. I. D. Jackson, eds., *Europe's Franco-German Engine* (Brookings, 1998).

21. See "Les déclarations du Président de la république," *Le Monde*, October 23, 1991.

22. Daniel Vernet, "Les Européens s'interrogent sur leur action au Kosovo," *Le Monde*, March 19, 1998.

23. On the confederation project, see an article by Mitterrand's foreign minister: Roland Dumas, "Un projet mort-né: La confédération européenne," *Politique Etrangère* (March 2001), pp. 687–703.

24. Robert Cooper, "The Post-Modern State and the World Order," *NPQ* (Special Issue, 1997), pp. 48–55.

25. This new French outlook was conveyed by Jacques Chirac in a speech before the U.S. Congress, Washington, D.C., February 1, 1996 (www.elysee.fr).

26. "[L'Europe,] en se dotant d'une capacité d'action militaire, devient un acteur politique complet." From President Chirac's speech to the Institut des hautes études de défense nationale, Paris, June 8, 2001 (www.elysee.fr).

27. John Mearsheimer, "Back to the Future: Instability in Europe after the Cold War," *International Security*, vol. 15 (Summer 1990), pp. 5–56.

28. Hubert Védrine, interview in the daily newspaper *Libération*, February 9, 1999.

29. Joint communiqué issued by President Jacques Chirac and President Jiang Zemin, Beijing, May 14, 1997 (www.elysee.fr).

30. Hubert Védrine, Discours au Club de la Bourse, September 29, 1998 (www. france.diplomatie.fr). Védrine expounds on his view of the challenge globalization poses for France in his book *France in an Age of Globalization* (Brookings, 2001).

31. Védrine, Discours au Club de la Bourse.

32. Ibid.

33. Intervention of Prime Minister Lionel Jospin at the Ministry of Foreign Affairs, July 23, 2001 (www.premier-ministre.gouv.fr).

34. Remarks of President Jacques Chirac at a press conference, July 13, 2001 (www.elysee.fr).

35. Hubert Védrine, Discours à la conférence de l'IFRI, Paris, November 3, 1999 (www.france.diplomatie.fr).

36. Ibid.

37. Christopher Caldwell, "Védrinism: France's Global Ambit," *Policy Review* (October 2000) (www.policyreview.com/oct00/caldwell.html).

38. Védrine, Discours à la conférence de l'IFRI.

39. Hubert Védrine, quoted in Olivier Gosset, "Europe: La politique étrangère commune aux abonnés absents," *Le Monde*, September 1, 1998.

40. Jacques Chirac, Discours à la conférence de l'IFRI, November 4, 1999 (www.elysee.fr).

41. "Chirac Says Vital for Clinton to Perform Duties Fully," *Agence France-Presse*, September 15, 1998. Chirac's call was prompted by the release on September 9 of independent investigator Kenneth Starr's report on possible grounds for Clinton's impeachment.

42. Jacques Chirac, Discours à l'occasion de la conférence des ambassadeurs, August 28, 1998.

43. This line of argument is developed by Jérôme Paolini in "The French Perspective" in Michael Brenner, ed., *Multilateralism and Western Strategy* (Macmillan, 1994).

44. Jacques Chirac, Discours devant l'assemblée générale de l'association du traité atlantique (ATA), Strasbourg, October 19, 1999 (www.elysee.fr).

45. Ibid.

46. Hubert Védrine, interview by José Luis Barberia, *El Pais*, FBIS Text, July 7, 1998.

47. Chirac, Discours à l'occasion de la conférence des ambassadeurs.

48. Hubert Védrine, interview, *L'Express*, January 28, 1999.

49. Alain Richard, interview, *Agence France-Presse*, January 29, 1999.

50. On this point, see Guillaume Parmentier, "Redressing NATO's Imbalances," *Survival*, vol. 42 (Summer 2000), pp. 96–112, esp. pp. 97–99.

51. The same pattern developed after the tragic attacks on New York and Washington on September 11, 2001. (On French reactions, see Philip H. Gordon and Bénédicte Suzan, "France, the United States, and the War on Terrorism," U.S.-France Analysis, October 2001, www.brookings.edu/fp/cusf/analysis/terrror.htm.) As in other times of crisis, France's instinctive reaction was to draw closer to its American ally. There was a remarkable outburst of spontaneous solidarity: the Elysée flag flying at half mast (very unusual in response to an event abroad); *Le Monde* being the first European paper to proclaim in its headlines the next day, "We Are All Americans"; and widespread popular disappointment that French forces were not involved earlier in the operation against the Taliban. (See "En France, l'antiaméricanisme structuré apparaît minoritaire et politique," *Le Monde*, January 6–7, 2002, citing opinion polls by SOFRES and IPSOS.) On the other hand, the government, and especially Prime Minister Jospin, was quick to stress that French participation in any operation would require full French involvement in its planning from an early stage. Statements attributing responsibility for the attacks to

faults in U.S. foreign policy began to appear in the press and on television within a few days. These views were fairly visible, although their prominence in the media far exceeded their importance among the public and in policymaking circles.

Chapter Three

1. Some observations in this chapter draw on Guillaume Parmentier, "Redressing NATO's Imbalances," *Survival*, vol. 42 (Summer 2000), pp. 96–112.

2. Frédéric Bozo, *La France et l'OTAN: De la guerre froide au nouvel ordre européen* (Paris: Masson, 1991).

3. David S. Yost, *NATO Transformed: The Alliance's New Roles in International Security* (Washington: United States Institute of Peace, 1998), pp. 28–35.

4. See Parmentier, "Redressing NATO's Imbalances"; and Gabriel Robin, "A quoi sert l'OTAN?" *Politique Etrangère* (January 1995), pp. 171–80.

5. On the U.S. view, see James Chace, *The Consequences of the Peace: The New Internationalism and American Foreign Policy* (Oxford University Press, 1992), pp. 70–82; Joseph S. Nye, "Redefining the National Interest," *Foreign Affairs*, vol. 78 (July–August 1999), pp. 22–35; Richard N. Haass, "What to Do with American Primacy," *Foreign Affairs*, vol. 78 (September–October 1999), pp. 37–49; David P. Calleo, *Beyond American Hegemony: The Future of the Western Alliance* (Twentieth Century Fund Books, 1987), pp. 215–20.

6. The French always like to point out that the first supreme allied commander in Europe was a Frenchman, Field Marshall Ferdinand Foch, during the First World War.

7. The Rogers doctrine argued that enemy forces should be engaged well beyond the front line in the event of enemy attack.

8. The Ministerial Meeting of the North Atlantic Council in Copenhagen, June 7, 1991, Ministerial communiqué, "NATO's Core Security Functions in the New Europe": "The Alliance is the essential forum for consultation among its members and the venue for agreement on policies bearing on the security and defence commitments of Allies under the Washington Treaty, as expressed in the Statement on NATO's Core Security Functions accompanying this Communiqué." See NATO website: www.nato.int.

9. François Mitterrand, *Réflexions sur la politique extérieure de la France* (Paris: Fayard, 1986).

10. George Bush and Brent Scowcroft, *A World Transformed* (Knopf, 1998), pp. 74–80.

11. Ibid., p. 74: "I had invited him to Kennebunkport specifically to give U.S.-French relations a fresh start, for in recent years they had been under some strain. There was often friction between the State Department and the Quai d'Orsay, but some officials in the Reagan Administration felt that Mitterrand, too, was difficult. Frankly, they disliked him and felt freer to speak out against him because he and Reagan were not close. I wanted to change this, and a private, quiet weekend in Kennebunkport could provide the opportunity."

12. George Bush and Brent Scowcroft, in their account of the Bush presidency, ascribe much of the blame to the French bureaucracy—and also to some extent to American officialdom—asserting that the decisionmakers on the political level had a better relationship. Much is made in the book of the excellent rapport between the two presidents, and of Bush's efforts to cultivate Mitterrand. However, this cannot gainsay the fact that projects pursued at the highest level in each capital were often incompatible. See also Roland Dumas, "Un projet mort-né: La confédération européenne," *Politique Etrangère* (March 2001), pp. 683–703.

13. Hubert Védrine, *Les mondes de François Mitterrand: 1981–1995* (Paris: Fayard, 1996). "By contrast, the future of NATO is, for the United States, the essential matter; one saw that during the reunification of Germany. They are determined to prevent, using the cover provided by the implementation of resolutions voted by the Security Council, that the Europeans mount in Yugoslavia an ad hoc form of intervention directed by them, which permits them to bypass NATO or to use it only as a provider of services. This side of their policy is crystal clear. (The fox does not like the grapes, but neither does he like the chicken to eat them.) For the rest, taking account of the fact that public opinion was only slightly aroused, it was enough for them to denounce from time to time, when CNN forced them to act, the 'cynicism' or the 'impotence' of the Europeans, 'the abominable injustice' of the solutions they put forward, and to dazzle the Muslims with visions of a lifting of the embargo (doubtless accompanied by vague promises of arms deliveries through indirect channels) in order to appear as more 'moral' than the Europeans, without engaging themselves on the ground. In terms of morals, this policy is rather cynical" (p. 657). "The President is trying to profit from the strategic revolution at the end of the 1980s to take up again and to advance the cause of a European defense. . . . The debate was finally joined on April 19, 1990, in Florida, at Key Largo. . . . That day, Bush and his effective and imperious Secretary of State, James Baker, had only one idea in their heads: to assure the survival and maintenance of NATO despite the end of the Soviet empire and of the division of Germany" (p. 729). See also Mitterrand, *Réflexions sur la politique extérieure de la France.*

14. Frédéric Bozo, *Two Strategies for Europe* (Lanham, Md.: Rowman and Littlefield, 2000).

15. Richard Holbrooke, "America, a European Power," *Foreign Affairs,* vol. 74 (March–April 1995), pp. 38–51.

16. William Pfaff, "After the Cold War, U.S. Foreign Policy Is out of Control," *Herald Tribune,* February 16, 1999; William Pfaff, "Europe–Etats-Unis: L'affrontement en vue," *Commentaire* (Spring 1999), pp. 87–95. For a contrary view, see Ted G. Carpenter, *Beyond NATO: Staying out of Europe's Wars* (Washington: Cato Institute, 1994).

17. Yost, *NATO Transformed,* pp. 73–75.

18. Mark Nelson, *Bridging the Atlantic: Domestic Politics and Euro-American Relations* (London: CER, 1997), pp. 37–40.

19. Jean Klein, "Interface between NATO/WEU and UN/OSCE," in Michael Brenner, ed., *NATO and Collective Security* (Houndsmills, Eng.: Macmillan, 1998), pp. 249–78.

20. Michael Mandelbaum, *The Dawn of Peace in Europe* (Twentieth Century Fund Press, 1996), pp. 45–65.

21. Pierre Joxe, Allocution à la cérémonie de clôture de la session plénière du cours supérieur interarmées, November 29, 1991: "The French-NATO accord ought to be revised to take account of the profound geostrategic transformations in Europe, for one thing, the affirmation of a European defense identity. . . . I soon will be, if one does not take care, the last defense minister in all of Europe not to participate in NATO meetings," quoted in Jacques Isnard, "La France accroîtrait sa participation à l'OTAN," *Le Monde,* December 4, 1991.

22. Louis Gautier, *Mitterrand et son armée: 1991–1995* (Paris: B. Grasset, 1999), chap. 2, pp. 77–96, and on this particular point, p. 81.

23. Richard Holbrooke, *To End a War* (Random House, 1998), p. 330.

24. Jacques Isnard, "Les efforts diplomatiques pour la paix en Bosnie—L'amiral Lanxade privé de réunion d'Alliance atlantique," *Le Monde,* April 28, 1994.

25. Such a move had earlier been advocated by French intellectuals. See, for example, Alain Finkielkraut, *Comment peut-on être croate?* (Paris: Gallimard, 1992).

26. Yost, *NATO Transformed*, pp. 286–91. See also Stephen M. Walt, "Why Do Alliances Persist and How Do They Collapse?" paper presented at the IISS 38th Annual Conference, Dresden, Germany, September 1–4, 1996, p. 16: "Not only will major external changes affect the leader's interests (and thus its willingness to pay a disproportionate share of the alliance costs) but the additional burdens of alliance leadership will eventually erode the asymmetry of power upon which such leadership depends." See also Paul M. Kennedy, *The Rise and Fall of the Great Powers: Economic Change and Military Conflict from 1500 to 2000* (Random House, 1987).

27. Hervé de Charette, "France for a Streamlined NATO: Setting the Record Straight," *International Herald Tribune,* December 10, 1996. See also his comments at a meeting at the Assemblée nationale, January 29, 1997: "If Europeanization of the alliance is brought to conclusion, then France will take its full place not only in the NATO structures it left in 1966, but in all the reformed structures that permit the Europeans to assume fully their responsibilities in matters of security and defense" (www. assemblee-nat. fr).

28. Charles Millon, "France and the Renewal of the Atlantic Alliance," *NATO Review,* vol. 44 (May 1996), pp. 13–16.

29. U.S. Representative Benjamin Gilman, Committee Report H. of Rep. 104–18, part 2, *National Security Revitalization Act,* February 6, 1995: "NATO is the only multilateral organization that is capable of conducting effective military operations to protect Western interests. . . . NATO is an important diplomatic forum for discussion of issues of concern to its member states and for the peaceful resolution of disputes. Admission of Central and East European countries that have recently been freed from communist domination to NATO could contribute to international peace and enhance the security of those countries." Senator Roth, Address to the NATO Summit Meeting, Madrid, July 8, 1997: "The first pillar is NATO enlargement, for which there is wide parliamentary

support. . . . [E]nlargement . . . will be an open and on-going process. The third pillar . . . concerns its structural adaptation to the post–Cold War world" (www.nato.int).

30. Bill Clinton in joint press conference with Jacques Chirac, February 1, 1996: "I told President Chirac how pleased we in the United States are with France's recent decision to move closer to the military side of NATO, a move that will strengthen our alliance and a move that is very, very important to the United States. I also welcomed the French efforts to build a stronger European defense identity within NATO. This will allow our European allies to deal more effectively with future security problems and spread the costs and risks of our leadership for peace, while preserving the basic structure of NATO." Public Papers of the Presidents—William J. Clinton—1996 (U.S. Government Printing Office), vol. 1, p. 121.

31. Nicole Gnesotto, "L'Union et l'Alliance: Les dilemmes de la défense européenne," Les Notes de l'IFRI, no. 2 (Paris: IFRI, 1996), p. 47.

32. Gilles Andréani, "France and NATO after the Cold War: Old French Problem—or New Transatlantic Debate?" Royal United Services Institute Journal (Australia) (February–March 1999), pp. 20–24.

33. Paul David Miller, Retaining Alliance Relevancy: NATO and the Combined Joint Task Force Concept (Institute for Foreign Policy Analysis, Tufts University, 1994), pp. 45–64.

34. Millon, NATO Review.

35. See Richard N. Haass, "The U.S., Europe, and the Middle East Peace Process," in Robert D. Blackwill and Michael Stürmer, eds., Allies Divided: Transatlantic Policies for the Greater Middle East (MIT Press, 1997), pp. 79–100.

36. Gilles Delafon and Thomas Sancton, Dear Jacques, Cher Bill: Au cœur de l'Elysée et de la Maison Blanche, 1995–1999 (Paris: Plon, 1999).

37. Ibid.

38. Thomas Sancton, "Why Can't We Be Friends?" Time, January 27, 1997.

39. Ibid.

40. Ministerial meeting in Copenhagen, June 7, 1991 (www.nato.int).

41. Declaration of the heads of state and government participating in the meeting of the North Atlantic Council ("The Brussels Summit Declaration"), Brussels, January 11, 1994: "We reaffirm that the Alliance is the essential forum for consultation among its members and the venue for agreement on policies bearing on the security and defence commitments of Allies under the Washington Treaty." Ministerial meeting of the North Atlantic Council in Sintra, Portugal, May 29, 1997: "This Summit [Madrid] will shape the new NATO as a foundation for the development of a truly cooperative European security structure as we move towards the 21st century." Madrid declaration on Euro-Atlantic security and cooperation, July 8, 1997: "3. While maintaining our core function of collective defence, we have adapted our political and military structures to improve our ability to meet the new challenges of regional crisis and conflict management." The alliance's strategic concept approved by the heads of state and government participating in the meeting of the North Atlantic Council in Washington, D.C., on April 23 and 24,

1999: "4. The Alliance has an indispensable role to play in consolidating and preserving the positive changes of the recent past, and in meeting current and future security challenges" (www.nato.int).

42. Miller, *Retaining Alliance Relevancy;* John Newhouse, *Europe Adrift* (New York: Pantheon, 1997), pp. 3–21.

43. Stanley R. Sloan, "Negotiating a New Transatlantic Bargain," *NATO Review* (March 1996), pp. 19–23.

44. William T. Johnsen and Thomas Durell-Young, "France's Evolving Policy toward NATO," *Strategic Review* (Summer 1995), pp. 16–25; and especially Robert P. Grant, "France's New Relationship with NATO," *Survival* (Spring 1996), pp. 58–80; see also Andréani, "France and NATO after the Cold War."

45. Pauline Neville-Jones, "Bosnia after SFOR," *Survival* (Winter 1997–98), pp. 23–24: "Americans need to remember that Europeans took a great deal of heat in Bosnia before the U.S. became involved on the ground; that a major reason why European efforts at peacemaking were doomed to failure was the ability of Bosnians to exploit the important policy differences between the U.S. and the European Union at that time; and that when the U.S. finally became active, it took over the policy process and has dominated it ever since. Who calls the tune pays the piper." As the political director at the British Foreign Office, Mrs. Neville-Jones participated in all the important meetings with the allies on Bosnia and was present throughout the Dayton negotiations. See also Jane Sharp, "Anglo-American Relations and Crisis in Yugoslavia (FRY)," *Les Notes de l'IFRI,* no. 9 (1998), p. 36: "American criticism was unacceptable to Europeans serving in UNPROFOR, however. Europeans resented American claims to the moral high ground when no U.S. troops were sharing risks with their European allies in Bosnia. Europeans also claimed—again with some justification—that Clinton's rhetoric slowed the peace process by encouraging President Izetbegovic to believe the United States would eventually intervene militarily on their behalf. Europeans believed that Izetbegovic's belief in a Clinton rescue operation discouraged the Bosnian leadership from cooperation with the international mediators from the EC and the UN" (p. 30); "on the matter of air strikes British policy was much closer to that of France and Russia than to that of the United States" (p. 36); "Rose's behaviour was widely condemned in the United States and in Germany" (p. 37).

46. Joseph Fitchett, "Despite Past Frictions with U.S., France Is a Full Partner This Time," *International Herald Tribune,* April 1, 1999; and Fitchett, "NATO Talks Buoy Kosovo Air Policy," *International Herald Tribune,* April 27, 1999. See also David S. Yost, "The New NATO and Collective Security," *Survival* (Summer 1998), pp. 135–60.

47. William C. Banks and Jeffrey D. Straussman, "A New Imperial Presidency? Insights from U.S. Involvement in Bosnia," *Political Science Quarterly,* vol. 114 (Summer 1999), pp. 195–217.

48. The French argument was spelled out most eloquently by Gabriel Robin, the former French permanent representative to NATO. See Gabriel Robin, "A quoi sert l'OTAN?" p. 176: "It is not absurd in itself to want to add to traditional NATO, to the

NATO of legitimate collective defense, a new NATO devoted to cooperation and the maintenance of peace. What leads to insurmountable complications, however, is to confuse the two and to superimpose one on the other; that is, to pretend to accomplish the missions of the latter with the means, in the structures, and in accordance with the spirit of the former; to do that is to pour old wine into new bottles. There is something embarrassing about the new NATO in accoutrements borrowed from the traditional NATO, something a little pathetic in its armor from a different age. The first makes one think of a whale stranded on the beach by a sudden, strong ebb tide; the other resembles rather one of those laboratory mice that is enclosed in a labyrinth and that vainly throws itself against the walls without finding the exit."

49. Jacques Chirac, discours du Président de la République aux ambassadeurs, August 29, 1996.

50. Hervé de Charette, North Atlantic Council, December 5, 1995: "France considers that it is time to rediscover the spirit of 1994. She is willing. The French authorities have decided to participate actively in the alliance's reform. The president has stated this publicly and clearly. In this context, I would like to state in what spirit we perceive the alliance's reform and what part France intends to assume in the process. I hope that this will make it possible to accelerate the momentum for change, thus facilitating France's full participation in a reformed alliance" (www.nato.int).

51. Miller, *Retaining Alliance Relevancy*, pp. 45–64.

52. Gabriel Robin, *Un monde sans maître: Ordre ou désordre entre les nations?* (Paris: Editions Odile Jacob, 1995), p. 278: "As to political leaders, they have been aware for a long time of the commodities that Europe offers them. It has, all at the same time, the appearance of a grand design and the advantages of an alibi. If Europe advances, one ascribes merit to it; if it moves timidly or retreats, it is easy to cast the blame on others. Even better, if it is necessary to make concessions in a negotiation, to bow before a ukase issued from Brussels, to sacrifice even an entire slice of national interests, Europe is there not to absolve what could be seen as a misplaced weakness but to transmute these transfers of power into acts of meritorious self-abnegation."

See also Guillaume Parmentier, "Security and Defence Policy: The Use of Flexibility," *EU Enlargement and Flexibility*, Conference Papers 23 (Stockholm: Utrikespolitiska Institutet, 1998); and "A Survey on France," *Economist*, June 5, 1999, p. 4: "For sure, France's chief postwar foreign concern has been the construction of Europe, and the main motive for this the peaceful containment of Germany. But, these days, French preoccupation with Europe often stems as much from its desire to stand up to the Americans as from its historical fear of Germany."

53. The Italian foreign minister, Lamberto Dini, stated without any consultation with the French that his country no longer supported the French position. See press briefing with Secretary of State Madeleine K. Albright, Rome, February 16, 1997: "We believe that AFSouth has worked very well. This is not only a question of the NATO command, there is also the Sixth Fleet. Also, in view of the importance this has for the Mediterranean, we believe that the redefinition of commands throughout Europe should

not involve AFSouth. This remains our position." See State Department press briefings archive on www.state.gov. In a joint news conference with William Cohen, Lamberto Dini also said: "We are encouraged by the fact that all other members of NATO would seem to consider this a reasonable approach to the problem. We are confident that also France may find it acceptable." "French Say No Deal Yet on NATO Command," *Reuters*, March 7, 1997.

54. Guillaume Parmentier, "Après le Kosovo: Pour un nouveau contrat transatlantique," *Politique Etrangère* (January 2000), pp. 9–32, and Parmentier, "Redressing NATO's Imbalances."

55. See comments of Lionel Jospin at the Institut des Hautes Etudes de la Défense Nationale, September 3, 1998: "France is actively involved in the effort of the alliance's internal reform: new command structures, relations between NATO and the WEU, the concept of Combined Joint Task Forces (CJTF). In this regard, France has announced that it will take its place in the permanent bodies of the general staff charged with planning them. Our association with the operational planning of NATO and the search for interoperability with our allies are corollary to our solidarity in the event of aggression as foreseen by the treaty and by our participation in crisis management affecting European security" (www.premier-ministre.gouv.fr).

56. Charles Grant, "European Defence Post-Kosovo," CER working paper, London: Centre for European Reform (June 1999). See also Michael O'Hanlon and Ivo Daalder, "Unlearning the Lessons of Kosovo," *Foreign Policy* (Fall 1999), pp. 128–40.

57. Some of the comments in the following section are drawn from Michael Brenner, "The European Union's Security and Defense Policy: NATO's Partner or Rival?" McNair Paper, Institute for National Strategic Studies, National Defense University (2001).

58. The benign attitude toward ESDP expressed by some senior U.S. officers reflects the hope that a better-armed set of allies could relieve them altogether of disagreeable missions as well as reduce the demands placed on overextended American forces to perform unconventional missions.

59. General Short's remarks were quoted in Michael Evans, "General Wanted U.S. to Call the Shots in Kosovo," *The Times* (London), January 27, 2000. The definitive account of the policy debates and strategic calculations by the Clinton administration is provided by Ivo H. Daalder and Michael E. O'Hanlon, *Winning Ugly: NATO's War to Save Kosovo* (Brookings, 2000).

60. Remarks by Minister of Defense Alain Richard, "Défense européenne et souveraineté," Paris, October 20, 2000 (www.france.diplomatie.fr).

61. Simon Serfaty, "France–Etats-Unis: La querelle permanente," *Relations Internationales et Stratégiques*, no. 25 (Spring 1997), pp. 52–59.

62. "Joint Declaration on European Defence," issued at the U.K.-France Summit, Saint-Malo, December 4, 1998 (www.fco.gov.uk).

63. Guillaume Parmentier, "After Nice: The Discreet Emergence of a Military Partner for the United States," U.S.-France Analysis, April 2001 (www.brookings.edu).

64. Guillaume Parmentier and Jacques Beltran, "L'identité européenne de sécurité et de défense: De Potsdam à Helsinki en passant par Saint-Malo et Pristina," *Annuaire Français des Relations Internationales*, no. 1 (Brussels: Bruylant, 2000), pp. 533–45.

65. Parmentier, "After Nice."

66. Final communiqué, Ministerial Meeting of the North Atlantic Council, Brussels, December 14 and 15, 2000 (www.nato.int).

67. Strobe Talbott, "The State of the Alliance: An American Perspective," North Atlantic Council, December 15, 1999 (www.nato.int).

68. Parmentier, "After Nice."

69. Resolution 208, passed by the U.S. Senate on November 9, 1999, did not include the stronger harsh language that the Foreign Relations Committee had approved earlier.

70. Jacques Chirac, Discours devant l'assemblée générale de l'association du traité de l'atlantique (ATA), Strasbourg, October 19, 1999 (www.elysee.fr).

Chapter Four

1. Robert Gilpin, *The Political Economy of International Relations* (Princeton University Press, 1987).

2. For insight into the French sense of their distinctive economic traditions and methods, see Maurice Levy-Leboyer and Jean-Claude Casanova, eds., *Entre l'état et le marché: L'économie française de années 1880 à nos jours* (Paris: Editions Gallimard, 1991).

3. Remarks reported in *EUROCOM*, vol. 8 (March 1996), p. 3.

4. To a lesser extent, authorizing the WTO's rule-setting and rule-enforcing powers for the sake of imposing order on the global marketplace restricts what the French government can and cannot do to influence its external trade. Colbert was the seventeenth-century French minister of Louis XIV who was largely responsible for the consolidation of state power in the monarchy. The institutions he established for generating financial resources and for building the country's economic infrastructure laid the intellectual and administrative foundations for the government's active direction of the French economy that continues, in modified form, until this day.

5. Hubert Védrine, *Les mondes de François Mitterrand* (Paris: Fayard, 1996), p. 751. Davos is the site of the World Economic Forum that annually brings together high-level government leaders, officials of international organizations, and academics for discussions of topical economic issues. Free-market economic philosophies tend to dominate.

6. Ibid., p. 47.

7. For an overview of the French perspective on the Uruguay Round, see "Multilatéralisme: Le GATT en crise," *RAMSES 93* (Paris: IFRI, 1993).

8. See Pierre Nora, ed., *Les lieux de mémoire*, Vol. 1: *La république: Symboles, monuments, pédagogie* (Paris: Gallimard, 1984).

9. The ability of French farmers to capture the sympathetic attention of the public was exemplified by the fame accorded José Bové, one of the leaders of the

Confédération paysanne (a radical farmers' union), the eccentric and colorful character whose protests against globalization in general and the American menace to France's agrarian culture in particular were punctuated by his championing of and participation in the dismantling of a McDonald's in the south of France.

10. Delors's role in the intricate commission politics over CAP and the Uruguay Round is discussed authoritatively by George Ross in *Jacques Delors and European Integration* (Oxford University Press, 1995), pp. 211–17.

11. Sharp clashes with Washington marked Leon Brittan's tenure as vice president of the commission with special responsibilities for the EU's extra-European trade later in the decade. Unknowable in 1992, these clashes did conform to his long-established attachment to the community and his dedication to promoting its legitimate interests. That simple truth, though, was lost sight of in the emotions swirling around the CAP reform issue in the hothouse atmosphere created by the GATT negotiations.

12. Peter Sutherland publicly expressed his views in "If GATT Fails, We All Fail," *Financial Times*, October 19, 1992.

13. This is the judgment of the authors based on personal interviews with Clinton administration officials.

14. Jospin vented his opposition in blunt public comments. They were reported in "France Rejects EU Plan for Trade Pact with U.S.," *Journal of Commerce*, March 13, 1998.

15. John D. Morrocco, "U.S., Europe Collide over Boeing Merger," *Aviation Week and Space Technology*, May 19, 1997.

16. Neil Buckley, Patti Waldmeir, and Christopher Parkes, "EU Threat to Boeing Merger," *Financial Times*, July 4, 1997.

17. "Agreement between the Commission of the European Communities and the Government of the United States of America regarding the Application of Their Competition Rules," USIA press release, September 23, 1991.

18. Brian Coleman, "U.S. May Retaliate if EU Rejects Boeing Merger," *Wall Street Journal*, July 18, 1997.

19. See the analysis in "Pascal Lamy: The EU's Trade Commissioner with a Finger on the Nuclear Button," *Economist*, July 7, 2001.

20. Remarks of Lawrence Summers, undersecretary of the Treasury for international affairs, G-7 Summit, Denver, Colorado, June 11, 1997 (www.g7.utoronto.ca).

21. Quoted in Gilles Delafon and Thomas Sancton, *Dear Jacques, Cher Bill: Au coeur de l'Elysée et de la Maison Blanche, 1995–1999* (Paris: Plon, 1999), p. 300.

22. "Le discours de Lionel Jospin," *Le Monde*, June 21, 1997.

23. "Denver Summit of the Eight," *Newsweek*, June 29, 1999.

24. The Clinton administration's efforts to soften the image of the United States created in Denver had some mollifying effect. Felix Rohatyn, who succeeded Pamela Harriman as U.S. ambassador to France, used his reputation and position to convey the message that "there is no American economic model that is the reification of a unique idea. It is the product of the country's geography, our history and our political evolution.

. . . There are more than enough opportunities in tomorrow's world for France, for Europe . . . to coexist with the supposed American challenge and for each to follow successfully its own path, in fixing its own priorities." Tactful words from a financier turned diplomat. Felix Rohatyn, "Washington and Paris, an Essential Partnership," *New York Times*, September 26, 1999.

25. See Lionel Jospin, Speech to the National Press Club, Washington, June 1998. "Contrairement à ce que nous avons affirmé, et peut-être cru, les créations d'emplois aux Etats-Unis ne sont pas seulement, ni même majoritairement, des emplois non qualifiés et des petits boulots" (www.premier-ministre.gouv.fr).

26. See Gerald Baker and Stephen Fidler, "O'Neill's World," *Financial Times*, February 25, 2001; and "First World Fundamentalism," Editorial, *Financial Times*, February 17, 2001.

27. Jospin would ruefully acknowledge that "the economy cannot be run by legislation and official texts. People must stop expecting the government and the state to take charge of everything," quoted in "Jospin to Fight 'Abusive' Layoffs," *International Herald Tribune*, September 2, 1999.

28. The first informed and most detailed account of the EMU project's eventful course is provided by Gabriel Milesi, *Le roman de l'euro* (Paris: Hachette, 1998).

29. Delafon and Sancton, *Dear Jacques*, p. 238.

30. Jean-Pierre Petit, "Euro Challenge to the Dollar," Comment, *U.S.-CREST*, December 25, 1998.

31. The ECB is not *their* technocracy, even though a Frenchman, Jean-Claude Trichet, is slated to head it for twelve consecutive years after the conclusion of Wim Duisenberg's half-term in 2002. Trichet, head of the Banque de France at this writing, shares the convictions of his predecessor. His relentless promotion by the French government expresses the hope that he will have a rationed native sensitivity to French national concerns—and thinking. The tenures of Messieurs Jacques de la Larosière and Camdessus at the helm of the IMF offer few clues, because they have operated in an institutional environment where French influence—intellectual and political—is far weaker than it is and will be in the EU. More important, the French authorities' point is that Duisenberg's appointment, because it was the result of a consensus of European bankers, lacked the political authority that prevails in the appointment of the chairman of the Federal Reserve or the president of the Bundesbank.

32. The most apocalyptic visions were offered by Martin Feldstein; see Feldstein, "EMU and International Conflict," *Foreign Affairs*, vol. 76 (November–December 1997), pp. 60–73; and Rudi Dornbusch, "Euro Fantasies," *Foreign Affairs*, vol. 75 (September–October 1996), pp. 110–24.

33. The tone was set in Lawrence Summers's testimony before the Senate Budget Committee, October 21, 1997: "If EMU is good for Europe, it will be good for us." 104 Cong. 2 sess. (GPO, 1997).

34. Jacques Chirac has stated repeatedly France's aim that a Euro-zone position be coordinated in advance of IMF and World Bank meetings. He wants the United States to

accept that as natural and "to understand that, with the emergence of the euro, we feel we now share joint responsibilities, along with the Japanese, for international financial governance." Quoted in Robert Graham, "Chirac in U.S. Overture on Foreign Exchange Policy," *Financial Times*, February 18, 1999.

35. Quoted by Jim Hoagland, "Globalism with a Human Face," *Washington Post*, October 11, 1999.

36. Quoted in Philip Shenon, "Republicans Hint Terms for I.M.F. Payment," *New York Times*, October 9, 1998.

37. As a result, France is probably the only Western country where in recent times an arms maker, Marcel Dassault, could become a national icon in his own lifetime, enjoying genuine popularity among the general public.

38. See Jean-Baptiste Duroselle, *L'abîme, 1939–1945* (Paris: Imprimerie Nationale, 1982).

39. See François Goguel and Alfred Grosser, *La politique en France* (Paris: Armand Colin, 1980), pp. 212–20.

40. See Pierre Dussauge and Christophe Cornu, *L'industrie française de l'armement: Corporations, restructurations et intégration européenne* (Paris: Economica, 1998), pp. 25–38.

41. Confidential memo of the National Assembly's Finance Committee, republished in *Valeurs Actuelles*, May 25–31, 1996. The preference of the Corps de l'Armement was nonetheless implemented.

42. The Communists, for example, always vote against increases in the military procurement budget and often advocate massive cuts, but they favor maintaining jobs in the defense industry and take great pride in its technological achievements, which they feel are due in no small respect to the industry's workers, including the large number who are organized in the Communist-dominated trade union, the CGT. In fact, the sectors of French society that are completely unsympathetic toward national military procurement are in a very small minority.

43. Ann Markusen, "The Rise of World Weapons," *Foreign Policy* (Spring 1999), p. 41.

44. See Dussauge and Cornu, *L'industrie française de l'armement*, pp. 79–110.

45. See Patrick Marx, "Après le NH-90, Paris et Bonn passent commande de l'hélicoptère de combat Tigre," *La Tribune*, May 22, 1998.

46. Jacques Isnard, "Selon le Congrès américain, la France a été le deuxième exportateur d'armes en 1998," *Le Monde*, September 10, 1999.

47. See Hubert Coudurier, *Le monde selon Chirac: Les coulisses de la diplomatie française* (Paris: Calmann Lévy, 1998), p. 131.

48. See Anne-Marie Rocco, "Washington encourage les alliances entre européens et américains dans la défense," *Le Monde*, October 27, 1999.

49. François Heisbourg, "Quels partenaires industriels pour l'Europe alternatifs aux Etats-Unis?" *Les Cahiers du CHEAR*, no. 40 (Summer 1998), pp. 7–18.

50. See Guillaume Parmentier, "Painstaking Adaptation to the New Europe: French and German Defense Policies in 1997," *Les Cahiers de l'IFRI*, no. 21 (Paris: IFRI, 1997), p. 35.

51. Ibid.

52. See Coudurier, *Le monde selon Chirac*, pp. 105–22.

53. See Ministère des Finances et de l'Industrie, "Regroupement des forces au sein de l'industrie nucléaire française: Renforcement du partenariat entre Alcatel et Thomson-CSF," Communiqué de Presse, July 29, 1999; Ministère des Affaires Etrangères, *Restructurations industrielles européennes*, Note, October 20, 1997; Philippe Gaillard, "Cinq questions sur le nouveau Thomson," *L'Expansion*, October 23, 1997; Jean-Pierre Neu, "Thomson-CSF: Le gouvernement choisit Alcatel Alsthom de préférence à Matra," *Les Echos*, October 14, 1997; Christophe Jakubyszyn, "Le gouvernement choisit Alcatel comme partenaire de Thomson-CSF," *Le Monde*, October 14, 1997.

54. See Anne-Marie Rocco, "La méthode Jospin appliquée à l'industrie," *Le Monde*, October 15, 1997; Alain Richard, "Thomson devra chercher d'autres alliances," *La Tribune*, October 14, 1997; Olivier Provost, "Alcatel et Dassault se déchaînent contre Matra," *La Tribune*, May 14, 1997, and "La 'grande Thomson' pour fédérer les forces d'électronique de défense," *La Tribune*, October 14, 1997; Philippe le Cœur, "Alcatel et Dassault plaident pour une recomposition française de l'armement préalable aux restructurations européennes," *Le Monde*, May 14, 1997.

55. See "Back to Its Roots: Europe's Third Largest Defence Company Wants to Build Bridges across the Atlantic as Cross-Border Collaborations Multiply," *Economist*, December 2, 2000.

56. See Olivier Provost, "Avec cet échec, le groupe Lagardère est contraint de jouer l'Europe," *La Tribune*, October 14, 1997; Alexandra Schwartzbrod, "Matra, la tête dans les étoiles," *Libération*, October 15, 1997; Jacques Isnard, "Selon Matra, la France tourne le dos à l'Europe," *Le Monde*, October 15, 1997; Jean-Luc Lagardère, "En voulant Thomson, nous voulions l'Europe," *Le Monde*, October 23, 1997; Manfred Bischoff, interviewed in *Le Monde*, May 16, 1997; Patrick Marx, "Lagardère trouve un allié allemand pour reprendre CSF," *La Tribune*, May 9, 1997; Patrick Marx and Nava Dahan, "L'allemand DASA choisit son camp," *La Tribune*, May 9, 1997.

57. See Serge Tchuruk, "Le groupe renforcé devient un acteur incontournable de la restructuration européenne," *Le Monde*, October 15, 1997; Olivier Provost and Bénédicte de Peretti, "GEC prêt à s'allier au 'nouveau' Thomson . . . que dénonce DASA," *La Tribune*, October 16, 1997; Vianney Aubert, "L'armement européen en ébullition," *Le Figaro*, May 9, 1997.

58. See Jean-Pierre Neu, "Le big bang européen," *Les Echos*, October 6, 1998.

59. See Vianney Aubert, "Aéronautique et défense: L'Europe en morceaux," *Le Figaro*, January 20, 1999; Alexandra Schwartzbrod, "Défense: Les Anglais font bande à part," *Libération*, January 20, 1999; Hugo Dixon and Alexander Nicoll, "How Project Super Bowl Won the Day," *Financial Times*, January 23, 1999; Ralph Atkins, "DASA Head Gloomy over Pan-European Defence," *Financial Times*, January 25, 1999.

60. See John Schmid, "European Aerospace Giants to Link," *International Herald Tribune*, October 15, 1999; Yolande Baldeweck and Vianney Aubert, "L'accord franco-

allemand relance l'Europe de l'aéronautique et de la défense," *Le Figaro*, October 15, 1999.

61. See Katia G. Vlachos, "Safeguarding European Competitiveness," Occasional Paper 4 (Paris: Institute for Security Studies, WEU, February 1998); and Frédérique Sachwald, "Banalisation et restructuration des industries de défense," *Les Notes de l'IFRI* (Paris: IFRI, 1999), pp. 37–41.

62. See Alexander Nicoll, "America in Its Sights," *Financial Times*, December 14, 1999.

63. "La politique française d'armement: Enjeu industriel, stratégie européenne, capacité opérationnelle" (Paris: DGA, June 1999); "Rapport d'activité 1998" (Paris: DGA, 1998).

64. See Emile Blanc, "Structure d'une industrie européenne de défense viable," unpublished Eurodéfense document, pp. 1–3; Jean-Michel Belot, "UE/Armement: Les ministres dotent l'OCCAR des moyens d'agir," *Reuters*, September 9, 1998.

65. Ezio Bonsignore, "OCCAR + WEAO = EAA," *Military Technology*, March 1997.

66. See Joseph Fitchett, "U.S. Signals New Openness to Transatlantic Arms Industry Mergers," *International Herald Tribune*, July 8, 1999. See also Thierry Gadault, "Les Etats-Unis autorisent les alliances transatlantiques dans la défense," *La Tribune*, July 8, 1999; Christophe Jakubyszyn, "L'industrie de défense européenne sensible aux sirènes américaines," *Le Monde*, June 15, 1999; "U.S. Advances Euro-Merger Policy," *Flight International*, July 21, 1999.

67. See remarks delivered by Deputy Secretary of Defense John J. Hamre at the American Institute of Aeronautics and Astronautics on May 5, 1999; "U.S. Seeks More Defense Technology Cooperation with Europeans," *International Herald Tribune*, June 14, 1999. For a pessimistic view concerning transatlantic mergers, see William Pfaff, "Transatlantic Mergers of Arms Industries Aren't On," *International Herald Tribune*, August 6, 1999. Gansler is quoted in "DoD Opens the Door to Transatlantic Mergers," *Jane's Defence Weekly*, August 4, 1999.

68. See interview of Manfred Bischoff, CEO of DASA, in "Dasa Chief Attacks U.S. Restrictions: Regulations on Sharing Technology Are 'Preventing Transatlantic Deals'," *Financial Times*, December 23, 1999. See also "Boeing Refusal to Order Warhead Alarms Britain," *Financial Times*, December 4, 1999, for reaction of BAe Systems to Pentagon decision to procure warheads from Boeing.

69. Gadault, "Les Etats-Unis autorisent les alliances transatlantiques dans la défense.

70. For example, see "Bischoff Asks Hamre to Clarify U.S. Globalization Stance," *Defense Daily*, July 30, 1999.

71. See "Prospects for Major U.S.-Europe Deal Dim, Execs Say," *Armed Forces Newswire Service*, August 5, 1999. See also Joseph Fitchett, "Trans-Atlantic Deals in Defense Don't Fly," *International Herald Tribune*, November 2, 1999.

72. "Prospects for Major U.S.-Europe Deal Dim, Execs Say."

73. John J. Hamre, Remarks at the American Institute of Aeronautics and Astronautics, American Forces Information Service, May 5, 1999.

Chapter Five

1. Jacques Chirac, Discours à l'occasion du 20ème anniversaire de l'Institut Français des Relations Internationales, Palais de l'Elysée, November 1999 (www.elysee.fr).

2. Richard Ullman, "The U.S. and the World: An Interview with George Kennan," *New York Review of Books*, August 12, 1999.

3. Philip H. Gordon, "The French Position," *National Interest* (Fall 2000), p. 64.

4. Joschka Fischer, "From Confederacy to Federation: Thoughts on the Finality of European Integration," Speech in Berlin, May 12, 2000 (www.jeanmonnetprogram.org).

5. Speech by President Jacques Chirac to the Bundestag, July 28, 2000 (www.elysee.fr).

6. Gilles Andréani, "L'Europe des incertitudes," *Commentaire*, no. 85 (Spring 1999), p. 36.

7. Proposals for elaborating and refining the New Transatlantic Agenda were presented by the EU Commission in a communication to the Council of Ministers: "Reinforcing the Transatlantic Relationship: Focusing on Strategy and Delivering Results," March 20, 2001 (www.eurunion.org).

Index

Aerospace industry: Boeing–McDonnell Douglas merger, 32, 81–85; European cooperation, 105–06; French, 104; helicopters, 105–06; military aircraft, 103, 106; U.S. government role, 81, 82, 85. *See also* Airbus Industrie; Defense industry

Aérospatiale, 81, 104, 105–06, 108

Afghanistan, 64

Africa, 24

Agriculture: CAP, 74–78, 80–81; in France, 75–76; trade disputes, 17, 74–78, 91, 97, 98; in U.S., 74–75, 78, 98

Ailleret-Lemnitzer agreement, 45

Airbus Industrie, 72, 81–82, 84, 90

Air transport agreements, 83

Albanians in Kosovo, 35, 62

Albright, Madeleine, 55

Alcatel, 112

Algeria, 41

Amsterdam Treaty, 113

Ariane, 72

Arms: common European policies, 113; export restrictions, 102, 114; exports, 101, 102, 105, 107–10, 114; land and naval, 107; missiles, 106, 110; nuclear, 9. *See also* Defense industry

Asia: economic competition, 73–74; financial crises, 26; relations with EU, 23

Aspin, Les, 56

Association of Southeast Asian Nations (ASEAN), 23

Automobile industry, 73

Balkans: contact group, 28; EU involvement in interventions, 20; Macedonia, 35, 37; NATO operations, 18, 42, 46, 59, 60, 62–64. *See also* Bosnia; Kosovo; Serbia

Balladur, Edouard, 47, 76, 77, 78

Bérégovoy, Pierre, 75

bin Laden, Osama, 28, 64

Blair, Tony, 57, 65, 89, 102

Boeing Company: competition from Airbus, 81, 84; government research and development funding, 81, 82; merger with McDonnell Douglas, 32, 81–85

Bosnia: Dayton agreement, 34, 35, 49; ethnic cleansing, 49; French policies, 47, 49; Implementation Force (IFOR), 59; NATO involvement, 46, 49; Stabilization Force (SFOR), 59; United